# The Unemployables

Thanks to Jo and all those who helped on the way:

All my family, those at Lewis Consulting Group (Simon Hill, Clive Booth, Roelof Iball, Ilona Hitel, Iain Halpin, Catriona Knowles, Elizabeth Williams, Melissa Davies, Diana Dixon, Arthur Forbes-Evans, Guy Laschinger, Jackie Pinnock, John Tuppeny, Simon Howe and Merle Marquis).

Thanks also to: Jimmy Price, Will Ricketts, Alison Blackburn, Derek & Hilary Fox, Chris & Jo Riddell, Phil & Kristen Harrington, Bob Nelson, Bill Dodd, Ian Hayward, Jenny Rogers, Linda Lee-Wright, Colin Collier, Jez Deacon, Edward Young, Richard & Amanda Mallett, Alan (& Deborah Norford-) Jones, Phil Stretton, Richard Jelfe, John Breakespeare, George Paxton, Gary Osborne, Paul Armson, Anil Kapoor, Simon Eccles, Paul Simpson, Anthony Finn, Helen Majerus, Evelyn Maass, Chris Brown, Patrick Walsh, Robert Postema, Fiona Price, David Price, Joe Price, David Northrop, Larry Fuller, Kaveh Atrak, Charles & Jackie Middleton, Martin Nelson, John Winnington-Ingram, David Kirkby, John Olliver, Alan King, Mark Stockdale, Chris Deering, Bill Thornhill, David Brown, Geoff Yates, Geoff Wilson, Steve Sorensen, Jos Adams, Ian Szerlowski, Fiona & Michael Ross, Gunther Heyden, Tony Loynes, Christine Lake, Stuart Rock, Mike Hewitt, Caroline Bankes, Tim Wright, Keith & Riva Elliott, David Hewson, Peter Footitt, John Dziobon, Jill Stone, Richard Hibbitt, Mia Ponten, Sid Bracewell, Peter Goldsmith, Nick Ericson, Chiew Chan, Simon Cowan, Rolf-Espen Olsen, Des Nichols, Calvin Booker and Kev & Trev.

---

Thanks also to those featured in this book who consider themselves to be 'unemployable'.

---

*Chris Lewis*
October 1994

# The Unemployables
## How top entrepreneurs achieved success

**Chris Lewis**

'It was clear to me that at an early age I was quite unemployable. I just seemed to have too many ideas, too much energy, too much ambition.' –
*Fiona Price, October 1992*

2000

Copyright © Chris Lewis 1994

All rights reserved. No part of this publication may be reproduced, stored in a retrieval system, or transmitted in any form or by any means, electronic, mechanical, photocopying, recording, or otherwise without the prior permission of the publishers.

First published in 1994 by Management Books 2000 Ltd
125a The Broadway, Didcot, Oxfordshire OX11 8AW.
Tel: 01235-815544  Fax: 01235-817188

Printed and bound in Great Britain by
BPC Wheatons Ltd, Exeter

This book is sold subject to the condition that it shall not, by way of trade or otherwise, be lent, resold, hired out, or otherwise circulated without the publisher's prior consent in any form of binding or cover other than that in which it is published and without a similar condition including this condition being imposed upon the subsequent purchaser.

British Library Cataloguing in Publication Data is available

ISBN 1-85252-225-9

# Contents

Foreword .................................................................................... vii

The Success Factors .................................................................... 1

The 'Unemployables' ................................................................. 19
    Doune Alexander-Moore – The Fighter ............................... 21
    Brian Angliss – The Racer ..................................................... 24
    The Rise and Fall of John Ashcroft – Whizz-kid ................. 28
    Douglas Bader – Hero and Villain ......................................... 33
    Andy Brown – The Student Entrepreneur ............................ 36
    Linda Beard – Designs on Success ........................................ 39
    Will Carling – Playing to Win ............................................... 42
    Bob Champion – Unassuming Hero ..................................... 47
    Shirley Conran – Superwoman .............................................. 50
    Keith Chorlton – The Right Stuff .......................................... 53
    Michael Dell – The Man Behind the Grin ............................ 56
    Daniel Field – A Cut Above the Rest .................................... 61
    Sir Ranulph Fiennes – 'The World's Greatest Living
        Explorer' ............................................................................ 64
    Richard Gabriel – Delivering the Goods .............................. 67
    Tony Gordon – Simple 'Self-belief, That's All' .................... 71
    John Harrison – The Wilderness Years ................................ 74
    Tony Hawser – The Successful Reject .................................. 77
    Howard Hodgson – A Passion for Life ................................. 80
    Grace Igwe – Mother, Teacher, Entrepreneur ...................... 84
    Colin Jackson – 'I'm Gonna be the Best and That's That' .. 86
    Sir John Harvey-Jones – Product of Empire ........................ 89
    Kevin Harrington – Reformed Troublemaker ..................... 92
    Lennox Lewis – The Importance of Not Being Afraid ....... 95
    Sophie Mirman – Typist Turned Tycoon ............................. 98

David Northrop – Waiter to Bond Dealer .................................102
Bruce Oldfield – No Problems, Only Opportunities.................105
Peter Parfitt – Laughing All the Way ........................................108
Bob Payton – The Great American Dream Salesman...............111
Jozsef Pinter – Beating the Really Red Tape .............................114
Fiona Price – Channelling the Energy ......................................117
Matthew Stockford – Captain Fantastic....................................121
Alan Sugar – Sweet and Sour ....................................................124
David Sullivan – Press On .........................................................127
Sir Marc Weinberg – The Barrister-Salesman ..........................129
Andrew Wilson and Tim Wilkinson –
  The Men with a Drink Problem ............................................133
Marco-Pierre White – The Recipe For Success .......................136

Appendix ........................................................................................139

The Unemployables Club................................................................143

# Foreword

There are many books about successful people. There are many tapes, videos, seminars and lectures on how to become wealthy. There are hundreds of 'successes' who will tell you (at a price) how they did it. So why should you want to read this book at all? Well, you've got this far on the basis of intuition alone, but where's the evidence that suggests you should read on?

This book is different in a number of ways. First, it makes no claim to impart the secrets of success through wealth. If that's what you're after, put this book down and go and get the one with the picture of the millionaire on the back. What makes people a success, despite the identifiable qualities, remains a mystery, because ultimately, whether someone wants to be a success is a matter of will power. Whether you want to do anything with your life is a deeply personal matter and you yourself must decide what you want to do with it. One benefit of living in a democracy is that if you wish to waste your time, then you can. No book on its own can ever make you a success, no matter what it promises. You can only lead a horse to water, you can't make it drink.

Secondly, success is very different from being wealthy, although the two can coexist. Wealth is just having a heap of money, but success is a state of mind – a choice between trying to be happy, positive and good, or the opposite. The pursuit of 'success' for many people is linked to the accrual of power, status and materialism. For those who see the world in these terms there can only be one question: 'Why?' Normally, people want status because it makes them feel important and special. Thing is, if they need status to feel that way, then they have to keep adding to it. When you haven't got a car a Mini is nice. When you've got a Mini, you want a saloon. When you've got a saloon, you want a Rolls Royce. This is the procession that capitalism works on – that whatever material things you have, you should be dissatisfied. Yet all the money in the world cannot make you happy; it can only make you comfortable in your misery. Real success factors have to come from within. They cannot be an expression of inadequacy in material terms.

Thirdly, this books lets you hear what successful people have to say. It gives you the context, but it lets you hear it straight from the horse's mouth. You can read a lot or a little at any one time and each case study takes about fifteen minutes to read. It tells you where they came from, what their formative experiences were, who they most admire and what their beliefs are. Some of the personal circumstances will no doubt have changed before the book gets to print, because their lives move so fast. The most important thing is to see what they achieved and what sort of personal style brings that achievement about. Unfortunately, it is difficult to capture the full strength of someone's personality in the pages of a book. Perhaps someone will make it into a TV documentary....

In the majority of cases, they are drawn from first-hand interviews with the subjects themselves. Unfortunately, Douglas Bader died before I had a chance to interview him, but he is such an inspiration that I wanted to include him. There are quite a few subjects in the book who have suffered from physical handicaps and I include those people because they are superb problem-solvers and embodiments of real fighting spirit.

But these case studies are for those who want the detail. You don't need to read all the book to get the gist of what it's about. You have to work very hard when you're reading a book. Hopefully, multimedia and CD-ROM will make it commonplace for people to really enjoy the message as well as the medium. Until then, you'll just have to put up with inaudible, monochrome ink on paper. If you don't want to work that hard for your information or you're too busy to spend your time reading, then just browse through it.

Fourthly, this book is not about business or about entrepreneurs (although they feature commonly). This book is about inspiration and as such it should appeal to all people who have an interesting in making the most of their life.

For anybody with any sense then, there is no choice. Once you have consciously made the decision, there is no alternative except to go wholeheartedly towards the light. It is no accident that all the planet's major religions are based on positivity – it's the only way to live. Simply decide to be happy. Once you do that, the rest is a by-product.

## *The Unemployables*

Meeting the people in this book, and seeing how they overcame such large problems, cannot be anything but inspiring. You cannot help but be lifted by them. When I started writing this book I had a broken leg and was told I could not do anything but read. I had never done any professional writing but I thought if I could read, then I could write, so I hit upon the idea of this book. Later, I figured if I could write, then I could drive an automatic car. Being bored one day I borrowed an automatic car and drove to a nearby airfield where the thought occurred that if I could drive, I could fly. I approached an instructor who thought it was a bit of a joke. He nevertheless said he was game, if I was. Three months later, I had a pilot's licence.

By then, I had half this book written and had already seen enough to know that I wanted to be like the people I had met. So I struck out on my own as a business writer. Within six months I had cuttings from *The Times*, *The Guardian*, *The Daily Telegraph* and a host of business magazines. This sounds like it all happened by magic, but it didn't. I had to keep trying, knowing that no matter how difficult it was, tomorrow would be easier.

Within a year I had a thriving business going and was hiring other writers. The more work we took on the more lucrative the business became, diversifying into a systems, finance and marketing management consultancy. Today I am lucky enough to run an organisation which has doubled turnover every year for six years, employs ten people and is located in Covent Garden in the heart of London, where I now live.

The people I have recruited are like the people in this book. They are great to work with. They have drive, energy, a sense of humour and bags of determination. It's like having the book brought to life. Nowadays, I'm just doing what I would do every day of the week and I'm lucky enough to get paid for it.

I include this, just so you know that this is not just another book by a preacher who does not practise his credo.

There will be many who, reading this, will think, 'Yeah, it's OK for him, he had money enough to learn to fly, blah, blah'. Not true, I borrowed most of it. People said to me at the time, 'What about the risk?' My question is what do people really have to risk? In business, you're not risking your life, you're just risking rejection. People can only say no. The people who make excuses are the 'Great Blameless', always coming up with a reason why they can't get up and do something. I sympathise with them, because there is no one to show them how. Many successful people keep a low profile, simply because they are too busy. Others avoid the media because 'they're the people that spend their time writing about what other people do'.

Well, we're not all like that. Having seen both sides of the fence though, I can sympathise with that view as well.

My suggestion for getting people motivated towards their own goals is to attract high achievers into government – after all, there are no qualifications required to become Prime Minister! Many people think, quite rightly, that too many business people in politics would be a bad idea. I agree. But there can never be enough people who inspire us in politics. If those people did exist in Government then, truly, the political idealists would be able to bring about their better worlds in socialism or capitalism. The inspiration in both theories breaks down because it is applied by people who lack inspiration.

Those who can create this inspiration are special, if only for one reason – they create hope out of despair and strength out of weakness. They know human ordeal and triumph. They know the midnight and the noon of life. They represent a beacon of the human spirit. That's why this planet is special. Not because it supports life, but because it creates hope.

To create real triumphs means exposure to potential disasters. It means taking risks, living life to the full – not in a reckless way, but in a way which maximises the skills innate in all humans.

This book therefore is not about 101 ways to be a success, nor is it a eulogy for capitalism (although that is often the most frequent outlet for talent). This book is about heroes and heroines who have chosen to live in a certain positive way and by doing so shine out amongst so much mediocrity.

Because success is available to all, and unconstrained by nationality, race, sex, ability, age or religion, the people profiled here come from many different backgrounds. The fact that they are winners does not mean that there are losers. Those who appear to lose are those who choose to do so, whether consciously or unconsciously. Nobody ever loses at anything, provided they are happy.

One last word from me. The people who destroy hope and happiness are the cynics. Watch out for them. They are everywhere, telling you how bad everything is and how you can never succeed. What they are doing is quite simple. They are travelling on the opposite continuum to you. They are spiralling down to the darkness and the negativity. One day they may stop and begin to go back up the other way. They will get you down if you let them, because they will have you believe we are all helpless. The easiest way to deal with them is to oppose them. If you're more diplomatic, you should just ignore them. Eventually, they may wake up to what they're doing wrong.

Unfortunately, there are no quick or easy tips to do as successful people do, but there are qualities they all display. The best way to see how they do it is to meet them. As not everybody can do this, a book is the next best way. I hope they inspire you in the same way as they have me.

# The Success Factors

Although the case studies of people in this book are entertaining enough, what follows here is my guide to the common denominators these people display. Of course, extraordinary people display lots of differing qualities, but it is clear when you interview such a cross-section of people that there are considerable common qualities between them.

You can get the essential facts by simply following the highlighted main points of this book. The thirteen points of being successful are positivity, quality, objectivity, tenacity, energy, flexibility, personality, individuality, consistency, creativity, honesty, luck(y) and factor 'x'. The main point, if you read no further is...

### Positivity — Choose to be positive about things

The next point is...

### Quality — Always think about improvement

That's another hallmark of success – always being interested in improving. The Japanese call it *Kaizen* and there has been lots written about it. But the basic truth is simple: success is not a destination. Those who think they have 'arrived' are doomed to disappointment. The real successes know what they have done is to recognise that the most successful thing is to travel *towards* success. Despite what all the success books say, it is simply a state of mind.

Our success factors cannot be a comprehensive list, because so many of the qualities these individuals have are personal. They appeal to different people because of the personal struggles they have overcome. Don't understand? Read on – all will become clear. You will hear the same qualities and issues mentioned several times over and you'll get the picture.

### Objectivity — Love of life, not money — Try to put money out of your mind

Love of money will no doubt bring an individual some money. But love of life above all gives the potential for real wealth. To really make money, you have to stop caring about it and concentrate on what you *really* enjoy doing. If you like what you do, you do it more. If you do it more, you get better at it than anyone else. If you're better than anyone else, you make more money. That's how the progression must run if it is to be successful in the longer term.

Money in itself is useless – but what it can do is precious. Some of the very successful people in this book would still do whatever they are doing irrespective of whether they get paid for it. That's why the money becomes unimportant.

It's also true that if you acquire your money in an underhand way it will bite you back, not necessarily today or tomorrow, but eventually. That's one of the few things you *really* can depend on. Many of those interviewed believe there is an emotional bank account which mirrors the financial one. Perhaps the most famous, if a little corny, example of this is Frank Capra's film *It's a Wonderful Life*, starring Jimmy Stewart. Stewart plays George Bailey, an ambitious boy who grows up in a small town. He gets many opportunities to leave, but each time he stays because he feels it's his duty. While his brother and friends leave and become wealthy and famous, he labours on at home looking after the family business. Then, on Christmas Eve one of his staff loses the company's savings and everything is put in jeopardy. Bailey decides to kill himself and is visited by a guardian angel who tries to persuade him that life is a wonderful gift. He does this by showing Bailey what life in the town would have been like if he hadn't been born. The town is shown as an unpleasant gin palace, where the sick and the old are uncared for and people are that much meaner. At the end of this depiction, Bailey can't stand any more of it and wants to live again. He returns home to find that all of his friends have rallied round to offer the missing amount and more. The message of the film is that one person's life touches so many others and that no one is a failure if they have friends.

The film has been networked in America every Christmas for many years and is immensely popular. Its popularity stands testimony to the way that people actually wish the world to be. For many of those people who have been successful, they believe life is like that, not because they have been lucky or privileged, but because they choose it to be that way. Some cynics would say that's naive, but what's best – to believe innocently in a better world or to believe stupidly that the human race is finished?

If you were privileged to search among some of the wealthiest people on the planet, you would find some of the most unhappy personalities. Why? Can you imagine living without the challenge of money? Can you imagine people simply wanting to get to know you because you had money? Can you imagine people hating you because you've got more than them? Can you imagine constantly having to think about security? Or people wanting to kidnap your children? That is the story of the world's super-rich. They are forced to live as far away from the masses as they can. They are suspicious of everyone. The ones who have enormous inherited wealth are amongst the unhappiest. They are pursued by the world's media. They can never rest or relax without someone being there to stick a camera up their nose.

Forget money. If you are successful, it will either come on its own, or you'll decide you don't want it.

## Tenacity — If you really want it, never, ever give up

Despite what many books say about the nature of success, it is never, ever instant. It may seem to be so but it is usually only the moment that the success is discovered. Even then, just because the media call it success, it may not be so. They are misled as often as everyone else. Also beware that if someone is successful because the media say so, what happens when the media suddenly start to call them a failure?

Often, the success has been there for many years before it becomes generally known. For this reason, one of the essential qualities of those who are acknowledged as successful is their ability to work for many years armed only with their belief in themselves or their ideas. Is this arrogance? Stubbornness? Singlemindedness? Or lunacy? It depends on your standpoint.

Whatever, recognition takes years to come, if it comes at all. If you're doing something for recognition, don't bother. Chances are it'll fail. You have to be happy with a fan club of one. Any more is a bonus.

In order to scale the heights, you have to be dissatisfied with the rung already reached. Remember, if you can do 'x', then you can do 'y'. You have to leap from bough to bough. Many of those interviewed in this book said they were driven to starting their own businesses partly because the pace of life in their previous companies was too slow.

This drive and ambition is like fire: a good servant but an evil master. In its latter form it can destroy health, wealth, relationships and the business itself. The first balancing act that most business people learn, therefore, is that the needs of the business must balance the needs of the body. The result of this has in many instances involved looking at how the body works and adjusting everything around it. Both Fiona Price and Howard Hodgson follow a diet known as the Hay system. This involves not mixing protein and carbohydrate at the same sitting, because one breaks down into acid and the other is alkaline, thus slowing down the digestive system. The stomach can apparently work more effectively if presented with one or the other. The result is that food is digested more quickly and the body can work more efficiently.

There is also substantial evidence to suggest that many use some form of alternative science to increase their ability, from meditation to the use of pendulums and dowsing rods to make business decisions – although few admit to it for fear of being seen as cranks. The upshot of this is that a game of respectability is played: trust and reputation are important qualities in business.

To succeed in business you must have a clear vision and set goals along the way. Perhaps David Northrop is the greatest purveyor of this skill, setting hourly, daily, weekly, monthly, quarterly and annual objectives. He puts these goals everywhere, so he is constantly reminded of them. He tells his friends and his family what he is going to do, so that they too will act as a spur for achievement. Last thing at night, he looks at what he wanted to achieve that day and reviews progress. Then he is into planning what's going to happen the next day.

This, contrary to what some people think, actually makes it easier to achieve goals, because you know what the next step is. What's more is that if you set goals for every day, you break down your lifetime goals into easily digestible chunks. That way going somewhere in your life becomes easier, not harder.

It is only by doing this that great visions can come into place and, inevitably, these take many years to achieve. Over that time, it is easy to become side-tracked or discouraged with progress and, for many reasons, give up. Strong planning and goal-setting help to increase determination to succeed.

They also have to overcome unforeseen challenges that everyone faces from time to time. Richard Gabriel is the best example of this. He suffered two office fires and a variety of bad luck instances. It just made him more determined to succeed. He mentions that in the depths of each tragedy there were always positive aspects to dwell upon. He mentions how fantastic his staff were when the fires struck. They worked long and hard to keep the company going.

While all of those interviewed knew a great deal about their own field of business, there were those who appeared remarkably ill-informed about the rest of the world. Many did not know who various government ministers were, who was at the top of the football league or pop charts, and current affairs knowledge tended to be poor.

This is because they spend more time creating their own success rather than reading about the success of others. Is this selfishness? Egocentricity? Or just quietly minding their own business? Most were media shy and astonished anybody might be interested in their activities, which they considered quite ordinary. At least that's what they said. Modesty does have a role here, too!

When someone is going all-out to achieve a long-term goal, they can often get wrapped up in themselves and gradually become quite ignorant of the way 'normal' people live. Because of this, they can sometimes seem remote and it can lead them to apply their own standards to others, assuming they have the same personal resources. This can sometimes lead to initial disappointment with human nature. It can also lead them into being all the more remote. Usually, however, because high achievers are such human optimists, it redoubles their drive.

Despite not having a great deal of time to watch TV or read newspapers, nearly all had specific hobbies which they undertook with the same verve as they did their business activities. Keeping pets was particularly popular. Fiona Price said that sometimes, after a day at the office, she liked to spend time with her horses because they were very relaxing and didn't talk back!

## Energy — Get fit, get organised, get busy

You can't achieve anything without physical, emotional, spiritual and mental energy. Everyone has more than they think. Winners are marked out by the amount of energy they have. This is measured not so much in the volume they have, but in how they apply it. Some display their energy in massive bursts at work, while at home they do nothing but collapse into a chair. Some have sprint moments while at work, but spend the rest of their time slowing themselves down. A few go like a rocket all day and all night for extended periods, then stop for a month in six to recover.

Whatever the style, hitting the right opportunity with the right energy is essential. Perhaps the best example of sheer personal energy was Bob Payton, proprietor of the 'My kinda town' restaurants. He was a man who frequently drank several cans of Coke for breakfast to start him up, followed by coffee. By ten o'clock he and his restaurants were buzzing and frequently stayed that way until two in the morning. He constantly looked like he was about to step into a ring and do ten rounds with Mike Tyson. The point he illustrated is that unless you do it yourself, you can't ask your staff to follow suit. Sadly, a few weeks before this book was published, he was killed in a car accident.

Energy is usually the one thing people run out of in business and all those profiled seem to have boundless depths of it. The reason for this is that the more you do, the more you become capable of doing. If you consciously try to go faster you end up going faster, unconsciously as well. Many successful people stretch themselves and develop what seem to be extraordinary levels of energy. In reality, this has been acquired over many years. This comes back to goal-setting. If the goals are small stepping-stones arranged in a line, it becomes easier to achieve slightly more every day. Compound this over time and the distance travelled is greater. One or two even said they made their energies more focused because they were naturally lazy and therefore when they did work, they wanted to be working in the most efficient manner. They knew they would never make it in business working for someone else because they were never motivated enough. It seems that for some people responsibility can really work as a motivator. It's difficult to look at somebody who has overcome a huge problem or built a million-pound company and accept that they think they are lazy.

Howard Hodgson, the funeral entrepreneur, likened it to having a demon on his shoulder who constantly nagged him. If he felt 'to hell with it – it'll do' the demon would nag him until the job was done properly. This is all the more interesting in his case, because until the age of twenty-five he was a hippy drop-out, who was more interested in pop music than business. Fifteen years later he had built a multi-million pound company and sold it. His book, *How to Become Dead Rich*, is worth a read in its own right. Again, he is a young man who has had the physical, mental, spiritual and emotional energy to overcome success, failure and significant personal tragedy in his life. When his son was killed in an accident, he translated his feelings of grief into setting up a charitable foundation. That's a *real* example of positive thought.

Energy levels are, of course, only relative to what other people have. However, they do count for a lot. All the people profiled said they did some form of exercise because it increased the amount of energy they had, advocating 'mens sana in corpore sano' (healthy body, healthy mind). In fact, everyone considered it absolutely essential for the long term to keep the body healthy. This is because they all make unusual demands on themselves physically, mentally, spiritually and emotionally. If this is maintained, there has to be a physical effect, eventually. John Ashcroft is a good example of this. When his business failed, he contracted hepatitis and was ill for three months. At its most extreme a life in business can be one of the most demanding challenges.

Everyone recognised health as being the Achilles' heel, because without a healthy body it was so much more difficult. Matthew Stockford is a classic example of this. There are many sick, old or disabled people who get depressed about their bodies, but the rule is to make the best of what you've got. The sheer physical presence of Matthew Stockford in a room is enough to embarrass the fitness of so-called 'able people'.

The most important point here is that no matter what state you are in, you can always improve. And if you contend that you are in the worst physical, emotional, spiritual and intellectual state, then you are going to have more fun bringing out your potential than people who are better off.

## Flexibility — Is this really the best way?

Flexibility among high achievers is an odd factor. In certain circumstances, these individuals display the most extraordinary levels of ingenuity and ability to work with the resources available. On the other hand, they have a fundamental inability to change who they are.

Flexibility is undoubtedly a key quality: too rigid an approach and something is forced to give. There are many stubborn and dogmatic people who fail to achieve things because they fail to see the alternatives.

Doune Alexander is an example of this. She was faced with a situation where she could not make her product in a factory simply because she could not afford it. So she didn't let this get in the way. She started up at home working in her kitchen. She couldn't afford staff either, so she enlisted the help of her family. She is a fighter by her very nature.

Timing is important here. Many achievers start out late in life, because they have always known what they wanted to do but were biding their time. Ambition can be fulfilled at any stage.

In any life full of achievement there is a cost. Sometimes costs have to be seen in the context of the happiness they create. There are few people in this book who have achieved their goals while being unhappy, emotionally or spiritually. In fact, for most the unhappiness is what motivated them to start out on their own. One person in the book admitted to never being 'happy' when he was happy. He knew that contentment would not last long before he had to look for another challenge. Some people call this insecurity: some call it appetite for life.

Everyone featured in this book was certainly only really happy when they were busy. Some had taken time off, sometimes as much as six months at a time. This, however, was only really a breathing space to allow them to recover. If there is one thing that unifies all the people in this book, it's their relative inflexibility to change who they are. For instance, they may be able to change their environment, their work methods, their approach, but they could never become motivated by a life of leisure.

This is perhaps the surest indicator of the sort of people who become successful. They are people who cannot live the way society asks them, therefore they change their environment until it supports the way they want to live.

If they pursue their goals to the exclusion of all else, then the law of diminishing returns creeps in. All entrepreneurs have been through stages where work has dominated everything. Superlative efforts forced them to sacrifice everything to reach the desired goal because their will would allow no other course. This usually causes mental and physical stress which forces them to exercise even greater control over their environment. All high achievers are in the end forced to adapt their lives so that outstanding performance does not happen at the expense of mind and body.

This, then, is another hallmark of success – the person who finds a way of adapting his or her life to be able to do things which others find hard. In some cases, this has meant hiring an army of people. In others, moving closer to work (in one case living above it!). However they achieve this adaptation, all have made time to include the things in their life which provide other forms of sustenance.

An odd thing about successful people is that they can seem quite relaxed when interviewed socially or talking in a pub. They seem to be like cars with an enormous number of gears: they can simply slip up or down a gear and accelerate or decelerate as required.

The key issue in flexibility is knowing when to be flexible and when to be iron-willed. There is little point being iron-willed about things that don't matter, partly because it irritates people and partly because it wastes valuable energy which might otherwise be used on more important tasks. There are those who would fight a battle every day of the week with people who do not matter. They just get known as the 'Mr Angrys' of this world. Those who are unable to be flexible inevitably end up being selfish and very few really selfish people become truly happy.

## Personality — Just be yourself

It is a moot point whether it is the success that creates character or vice versa. What is clear is that those people who overcome problems to achieve are generally very likable characters. It is inevitable that high endeavour will involve many other people and high achievers are usually those with considerable people experience. They are fun to be around, they are positive and they are full of energy. Of course there are those who appear to be superficially severe and Alan Sugar is a good example of this. Sugar's severity, though, is merely a front. He is very busy and does not suffer fools easily. People therefore approach him only when they are prepared and when they have their ideas and thoughts marshalled. He does not like to waste time. His family life, of which he is secretive, is of great importance to him. He leaves work every day before six in order to be home with his kids, or playing tennis with friends.

Many of the people profiled here have been successful in business. Successful business people are usually perceived as being exploitative, unpleasant and greedy. Certainly those types get noticed, but they do not represent the characteristics of the truly successful. The sort of personalities that succeed are those that inspire people and the only way that can be done is by making people feel good. If they feel negatively about the person and what they are trying to achieve, they will not be committed to the task.

If there is one sad thing about the personalities of achievers, it is that they are seldom seen. They are usually far too busy getting on with their lives to comment on it. That's why many of the people here tend not to be internationally famous. They don't court media attention because it's not important to them. This is perhaps the greatest tragedy of all, because those who do court it often do so for selfish reasons.

The majority of these people do not seek media attention – they also don't seek to work with government. Sadly, these are exactly the sort of people who should be in government. They inspire a natural respect, they work hard and they have vision which inspires people of all backgrounds by example. Unfortunately the diplomacy and political correctness that are required in officialdom repel an 'unemployable'. Perhaps it is time we measured our career politicians against their achievements.

How you describe some of the personalities in this book has been the greatest challenge of writing it. How can you describe how a tiny person like Sophie Mirman or Doune Alexander-Moore electrifies a room with their presence? Howard Hodgson is so cool he doesn't sweat – he gets condensation. Marco Pierre-White makes women swoon because of his sheer *romantique* quality. Sir Marc Weinberg is extraordinarily polite and is charm personified. Some people, like Joszef Pinter, do it by being not what you'd expect. He wouldn't be out of place in a Northern working men's club, but in actuality he's more sophisticated than a Mayfair dinner party. Whether this is deliberate or accidental is difficult to say. There's no doubt that some people deliberately want you to think one thing so they can start off by destroying the image.

It is certainly true that success breeds success. Some people are able to ride a wave of popularity. People close to high achievers often comment that they are exciting to be around, or they are filled with energy when someone is around or simply that they just like being with them. It's easy to understand how Peter Parfitt does it and perhaps he is the best example. He looks as if he's having fun all the time. He walks around as if he's just heard the funniest joke ever invented. The really worrying thing in his case is that he usually has!

## Individuality — Never follow the crowd

Closely linked to the personality is the sense of individuality. The people in this book know themselves. As one put it: 'If you work for yourself, you soon get to know the Boss very well.'

In order to achieve, you must be prepared to stand up for your ideas and beliefs. This means that you must be an individual. This means standing out from the crowd and being prepared to tolerate loneliness – the latter feeling tends to last only a short while. Daniel Field, the hairdresser, did exactly this. At school he was called a 'pansy' because he was interested in hairdressing. He was vilified and bullied for doing what he really wanted to do. Nevertheless, he stuck at what he enjoyed even though it meant losing some friends.

Many in this book have related how isolated they felt when they first decided to stand up for what they believed in. Sometimes this meant parting company with friends, lovers and wives in order to achieve a dream. Most say this would have been inevitable eventually because if the dream was more powerful than the relationship, then the latter was not good enough. Some say that they simply feel happier on their own.

Being a real individual is a lot harder than it would seem. When something goes wrong in a venture, as it inevitably does from time to time, there is no one to help. This can be the loneliest moment in anyone's life. Fortunately, those who strike out on their own often find other people who are following a similar path. Many described that one of their most formative experiences was shortly after they started up on their own when they met someone else who had done the same thing. They knew they could do business together because they recognised the qualities each other had. It also helped them to understand why it seemed they were alone – because the other successful people were also busy getting on with it rather than looking around for others to help. The habits of the successful are by their very nature personal and not publicly displayed.

One odd thing about achievers is that they often follow a path that is new to them, but has been trodden by many others in advance of them. There is, however, no school for this and no club that encourages it. None of the existing business institutions is geared up for it: they choose to focus on management or directorial status. None of the universities teaches entrepreneurship or achievement even though there is a clear set of skills involved. There is simply nowhere to learn how to become the best. Why is this?

For that reason, a club has been formed called the Unemployables Club. It is for entrepreneurs and other achievers to meet and exchange ideas and views. We hope that from this, other roles will spring. The details of this are on page 143.

But you don't have to join a club to set a course for success: just believe that all entrepreneurs have failed at something and have been told they were no good. Failure just serves to make success sweeter.

## Consistency — Stick at it!

Consistency is similar to tenacity, but some people can be tenacious in their approach and inconsistent in their attitude. To succeed at anything usually requires that the person be consistently outstanding, otherwise the success goes unnoticed or is very short-lived. Marco Pierre-White is a good example of this. Although on the surface he appears volatile and temperamental, his underlying approach is totally consistent. He believes in quality service in his restaurant. This doesn't just apply to the food but to the service, environment and booking procedures.

Perhaps the greatest exponents of consistency are the Japanese. They believe that consistency can be achieved only by continual development. Consistency in English means staying the same, but the Japanese believe that to stay the same is tantamount to slipping back. This principle is embodied in the Japanese word *kaizen*, which means continual improvement. From the outside it looks like consistency but from the inside it means continual meetings and discussion on how things can be further improved.

Consistency is perhaps the most underrated and least visible of all of the qualities required by winners. It is not spectacular and the only way it can be spotted is over time. This is because it is dull; it is mundane; it is the many times, night after night, when someone comes home late from work. It is the extent that someone goes to to make sure that a customer gets really good personal service. It's the sort of mind-boggling detail that makes sure that every glass in a restaurant is clean. It's the sort of approach that constantly looks for the best people and trains them to be better.

This illustrates an important point about those who would search for 'jobs'. Everyone in this book cited people as being the most important ingredient in what the company did and they were constantly on the lookout for promising staff. All had seen lots of CVs from hopefuls, but equally they all said they were mainly poor quality. They said they seldom got people phoning after they had sent their CVs and certainly never just turning up. There are few who would refuse to see someone who turns up in person to show how they can add value to a company; indeed, this is how Marco Pierre-White got his first job.

This is perhaps the brutal truth of searching for a job. You have to be able to demonstrate that you can make or save money for an employer. It is education that fails business in this respect. The statistics for unemployed students stand testimony to the fact that not only is education not giving the skills that businesses need, it is not giving the basic skills that enable the skills to be sold. These skills are still learnt by trial and error.

There are several things successful entrepreneurs do consistently and looking for people is one of them. Laughing at the question, 'Where do you want to be in five years' time?' is another. No entrepreneur knows that. As Alan Sugar succinctly put it: 'Anyone that talks five-year plans, talks crap.' They all want to be free to be able to take opportunities. They all want to remain opportunist. They want to remain consistently free.

If you have found a way of life which is natural enough for you, you will stick at it because it will be modelled around how you live.

That makes it easier to develop the habits that will make you successful.

## Creativity — Keep the ideas flowing

Part of the zest for living that so many successful people have is embodied in their creativity. This is not just artistic creativity, but intellectual, emotional and spiritual creativity.

All of those profiled have had to be creative in many different ways. To lead people requires nothing less. It means simply the ability to keep an idea alive and refreshed with constant input and energy from all sources. Tony Gordon, who has been feted as a brilliant salesman, is constantly refreshing his approach with new ideas that come from discussions with friends, colleagues and customers.

Most of the people in this book are constantly reinventing themselves and their approach to their work. They do this by reading about what others have done, although many expressed concern about the content of many of the self-help books. A few said they felt that the importance of self-help books was not so much to educate a new technique but to get the mind thinking about what could be done from another angle.

There are several cases of successful people spending time mastering new techniques to allow them to learn faster or more thoroughly. Quite a few had learnt speed reading techniques such SQ3R (Survey, Question, Read, Recall, Review). This simply involves shifting the focus of one's reading away from the actual reading to the point of the task. Therefore the person surveys the text, asks what they want to know about it, then reads it lightly before trying to recall and review the process. Readers are asked to vary the speed at which they read according to the complexity of the text. Others had consciously thought about the environment in which they felt more comfortable thinking or studying. Some even had favourite foods they would eat in order to get their creativity going. (Chocolate is the most common, if you're wondering.)

Many of those interviewed had specific techniques for boosting creativity. These ranged from the use of transcendental meditation through to the use of pendulums. Of course, there were plenty of mundane problem-solving techniques such as taking the dog for a walk or sitting in the bath. There is a general law at work here though: it seems that the greater the achievement, the more finely honed the individual is. For this reason a disproportionate number seem to be interested in the alternative sciences.

What do I mean by alternative sciences? Since you ask: anything which is not recognised and quantified by Western science. Because of the crankiness associated with this issue, it is not possible to identify individuals; suffice it to say that several were making and influencing decisions with pendulums, radionics and what might be called 'the power of positive thought'. Many know these techniques work, but don't why. One said that when he wanted new business, he just thought about it and imagined that the customers he wanted were phoning him to give him new orders. Lo and behold, it happened. He had done this so many times it couldn't be coincidence. Yet everyone has had the experience of thinking about someone before they suddenly call. This is the intuitive power and it is recognised openly by almost all successful people. Some described their intuition as being like praying. Some feel it just happens on its own on a long drive. Some just get a miraculous solution to a problem when they are in a relaxed place, like the bathroom.

It was the philosopher Carl Jung who first talked about the concept of the 'collective unconscious'. This, he said, was what people tuned into when they were praying collectively and also what they accessed when they were in the meditative state. One thing is for sure, many successful people use meditation, conscious or unconscious, to solve problems and put things in order. Fiona Price described this in a very simple way. She feels the modern world is so full of distractions that we spend most of our day exposed to – television, radio, newspapers – that the very pace of life means people do not spend time simply doing nothing. When anyone does that in a quiet room for twenty minutes or so, it gives them a chance to relax and to consider a few of their worries or questions.

It works like this. Switch off any noise and go into a room where you will not be disturbed. Sit on a chair with your palms turned upward, resting on your knees. Take three deep breaths and hold each one for ten seconds before breathing out. Then try to empty your mind. Try to think of nothing. Some people find it helps to stare at a flower or a candle or just out of the window. It will seem at first as if nothing is happening, but try doing this for two or three times and you will begin to feel a subtle benefit of being slightly better throughout and calmer.

Many, at this stage, will be shaking their heads sadly, but a lot of the mumbo-jumbo is based on common sense. You have to think positively in business to succeed. Everybody agrees that. Keeping fit is also sensible, as is maintaining a good diet. But perhaps the best rule to apply is that if it works for you, then fine. One thing is for sure, successful people have to maintain a creative approach to every aspect of their life. They cannot rely on everything their parents taught them, partly because the pace of the modern world is something that no one was ready for.

The most valued aspect of creativity, however, was universally agreed on: people again. Sometimes they can be brought together so that as a group they come up with better ideas than anyone singly. There are lots of techniques for coming up with ideas. Suffice it to say that the entrepreneur's creative side has an important part to play. It is the side from which ideas to solve problems come from and it is in use every day. It goes without saying that all successful people are interested in creativity and genuinely creative people. These don't have to have ponytails or hang out in advertising agencies. Despite the public image, you meet as many creative brains dressed in suits as you do in 501s.

## Honesty — There are no shortcuts

Honesty is not just the best policy – it is the only one. To really succeed requires not only honesty with others, but honesty with yourself. This applies especially to people who have been successful and who have lost their original creation. They have been frank with themselves and learnt from their experiences. Some people, however, do not learn from their experiences simply because of pride, arrogance, ignorance or lack of honesty. Any form of success requires that truths be faced up to. Sophie Mirman is a good example of this. She and Richard Ross formed the internationally famous 'Sock Shop' only to have it go bust within a few years. This did not stop them, however, from going into their following venture with greater experience and just the same enthusiasm.

If you believe in something and you are honest, then other people are likely to follow you. If you cut your business partners or your customers a bad deal, they will remember and they will tell their friends. A reputation is one of the most important assets a successful person can have. The principle is called 'win-win'. How do you, and the people you're working with, both get what you want? If you think this way, you're unlikely ever to have the feeling that you're playing on a different team. If you have the feeling that you're putting one over on the customer, your staff or your partners, you will eventually end up in trouble.

Everybody profiled said they would not do anything that was knowingly dishonest because they believed in the principle of what goes around, comes around. This does not stop the press picking up certain things that have been done by achievers and twisting them. The best example of this is Keith Chorlton, who rose from a poor background to become a wealthy entrepreneur. As with many achievers, he has had failures and made errors of judgement, but to many elements of the UK press this is unforgivable.

This again accounts for the fact that few achievers seek media attention. They know that once a story about how good you are has ceased to be fresh, then another about how bad you are must be on the way. In some respects this is just part of the world of journalism, as newspapers have constantly to find new angles on stories to keep the reader interested.

Somewhere along the line the media have given the public the idea that successful people must have done something underhand to get their wealth. These are the ideas of the 'Great Blameless' – that somehow, somewhere, someone might actually be cleverer or more talented than they are. The other phrase here is: 'You only need to now what God thinks of money by who he gives it to'. Well, this is partly true. Really wealthy people do not rub your face in it, because to them it's quite natural, therefore what's the big deal? It's only those people who are unused to wealth that need to display it. There are some good people with money and many of those have made it themselves. One thing is for sure, if you make your money dishonestly, it will come back and haunt you – not least because people will know and will resent it. Being successful is a position of responsibility. If you misuse it, people will resent it.

Money or no money, the same principles apply to rich man or poor man. You have to do right by people.

### Luck(y) — Make your own luck

Luck is a strange thing. There is an old line, often repeated, which came from Gary Player, the South African golfer, who once said: 'The more I practise, the luckier I get.' No doubt there is an element of this in most people's lives; however, it is undeniable that some people just do seem to get the breaks. But this is because they plan for opportunity. This may seem to be a contradiction in terms, however: opportunities can be taken only if the individual has the resources available.

Some people said that Will Carling, the England rugby captain, just happened to be in the right place at the right time. That, however, is not the whole story. Carling was very mature and very ambitious for his age and worked hard to get himself fit. Furthermore, when he came into the team he was very young compared to the older hands and had to earn the respect of those around him. He set about this through leading by example and acting as a source of inspiration for others. You cannot succeed by being a prima donna; people have to respect and believe in you. Some people call Carling's career lucky, but when he was in the right place at the right time, he was ready. Is that luck?

Linda Beard was also young when she first won success. Design, of all areas, is highly competitive and difficult for young people to get into. It's clear from talking to her that it was her considerable personal charm allied with a huge capacity for hard work that marked her out at an early stage.

The other thing about successful people is that because they are so tenacious, they never miss opportunities. They simply make sure that when the opportunity comes up once in a lifetime, they grasp hold of it and don't let go.

This is all very well, but it doesn't explain how some people seem to have a charmed life. There seems to be nothing to explain why some people seem to be able to avoid personal disaster by inches or minutes, but many of us totally underestimate the skills and tolerance that some very able people work to. In many cases they are using innate, unconscious skills and abilities that can only really be guessed at.

## The 'x' factor — Believe in yourself

With all successful people there is usually an additional factor which catalyses all other characteristics. Usually this is an event, sometimes it can be another person, but nearly always, while the talent is there, for many people it takes something to bring it out. Nobody can give you confidence or self-belief. Suffice it to say that to succeed in Britain is difficult because so many people are competing for the same opportunity.

In many instances success or failure is dictated by the reaction that people have to a disaster. Matthew Stockford embodies this. When anyone talks to him about breaking his back, he makes it sound like he stubbed his toe. That is how he has made himself think about it – he reduced it in his mind to an insignificant point. It is impossible to be in the same room as someone like him and feel sorry for yourself because you have a cold. People like Stockford put the minor niggles of life into perspective. People moan about their lot, having to walk to work or look after the kids, yet so many are denied the privilege.

How some people are able to handle ever greater challenges while still being relatively inexperienced is difficult to understand. This brings us back again to the issue of alternative sciences. A few of those profiled said they ascribed their considerable life skills to having lived before. Before you fall out of your chair, it's worth keeping an open mind. Many described the feeling of having made the same sort of progression before. Further investigation revealed that the names of some regressive hypnotherapists were passed from person to person as being particularly good. Underneath the conservative exterior, there are many successful people who believe in things that would make those who follow them question their authority or credibility. That's why nobody likes to talk about it, but it doesn't stop them practising it. Perhaps, at some stage in the future, we might all become open-minded enough to investigate what lies behind some of these strange beliefs.

The even funnier thing about all those who are profiled in the coming pages is that none of them think they should appear in a book of this kind. They see nothing extraordinary in what they do. When all the praise or criticism has been heaped upon them, they are just what they are.

The last bit of advice:

**No excuses — Just do it!**

# The Unemployables

## Doune Alexander-Moore – The Fighter

If you want anything in this life you have to be prepared to fight for it. That's the lesson that all successful people preach. Doune Alexander-Moore is an exceptional example of the principle in action. She's black. She's small. She's divorced. She lives in London's East End and has brought up two young daughters on her own. As far as minority groups are concerned, she has blanket membership. But that has not stopped her. She fights with the strength of ten men.

Her struggle started earlier than planned. Forty years ago, babies born three months premature weren't expected to survive. But Moore's grandmother, a Caribbean herbalist, told her mother that the baby had come to stay. With the help of Gramma's ancient wisdom, she grew up to be the strongest and fittest member of the family. Then, in her teens, she left the Caribbean to come to England – the England she'd heard so much about in textbooks.

What she wasn't prepared for was the racism and prejudice she found here, not so much among the British people but amongst the authorities. 'I have never had any problems with the British people at all. Wherever I've worked in the past, I've always been the only black and I've always been treated with respect. I'd never really experienced prejudice until I set up in business.'

Moore puts it down to ignorance and stereotyping: 'Number one, I'm a woman, number two, I'm black. I live in a council flat. I have no money or collateral.' The business she started to market hot pepper sauces is growing rapidly. Yet its managing director still has difficulty persuading a bank to provide her with an overdraft facility. 'I've been invited to register for public appointment by the Cabinet Office and I advise government ministers. My expertise is good enough for them, but it is still not good enough for the British banks and financial institutions,' she says.

Undaunted, she battles on without financial backing. 'I didn't know it was going to be such a big job, but I think it's like anything in life: you start off in ignorance and you learn as you go along.'

However, her determination to fight injustice has enabled her to triumph over circumstance: 'I started the business during the lowest period of my life. My marriage had broken down and I was left with my two young girls in a council flat. For the first time in my life I was living in shared accommodation and I was totally broke.'

She had no other way of earning a living until her daughter suggested selling her sauces. 'I'd been making them for years, and I'd always had a lot of my friends buying them from me. It was just like a hobby, because I was brought up with it. Hot peppers are a natural flavour enhancer, but they also revive and refresh every part of you. There are others on the market, but they are western adulterations of the real thing. These are original Caribbean hot herbal sauces.'

Her faith and knowledge in herbalism and natural foods enabled her to treat her daughter, who was born with a hole in her heart and as a result is very prone to colds. 'I make her hot toddies with hot peppers, honey and lemon. I've never given her cough medicine, but with my kind of medicine she is well in a day. Part of my message has always been that natural foods are our best medicine.'

Whether for fitness or flavour, her sauces are in demand in some of the best department stores in the country, including Harrods and Fortnum & Mason. 'I just went along and explained why they tasted so good and what went into them,' she says, having also persuaded seven major supermarket chains to carry her products. She has plans to move into the Republic of Ireland, and Spain is also on the agenda. A faithful band of 'guinea pigs' around the world have been consumer-testing new products which she intends to launch.

'It's taken a long time. I do everything myself, from product and packaging design through to labelling and promoting. I deal with the wholesalers and distribute the sauces myself. I think quality is the most important thing, and it's never, ever been questioned.'

But, as they say, success has not changed her: 'I still look at myself as an ordinary working-class woman. I get invited to all kinds of functions. I have made personal friends with many top ministers and celebrities, and even been recognised by Princess Anne. It's such a nice feeling to have someone notice your hard work. It's hard to believe, I used to be ultra-shy.'

Public recognition was inevitable. Moore is a natural communicator, a one-woman publicity machine. Her experience, in this as in other areas of business, is that persistence pays: 'I figure that if I send out press release after press release, sooner or later they'll be interested enough to find out who this woman is who keeps pestering them. I've always used my womanly wiles. There's one thing a man can never beat, and that's a nagging woman!' In five years she's appeared in 28 TV programmes, more than 50 radio shows and in 170 national press features.

## The Unemployables

Obviously there have been hard times for her over the years, but she is buoyed up by the philosophy handed down to her, like the secret recipes for her herbal sauces, by her grandmother: 'We arrive here with nothing and take nothing away with us. The most we can do while we're here is live in harmony. Unless you keep your feet on the ground, you can be carried along by trends. To have survived the worst and to achieve beyond your dreams, takes hard work.'

Her success has not come without sacrifice: 'It's taken seven days a week. My Mum says she's never known anyone who can work as much as me. But I also practise yoga and meditation. When I sleep I have concentrated sleep.' (Moore keeps a deckchair in the factory, so that when she is really tired, she can take a couple of hours' siesta before starting work again.)

'We normally finish there at six. Then I go home and start my paperwork and carry on until about one in the morning. Hard work is what it takes for anyone to succeed. Unfortunately, commitment and dedication no longer seem to come up in the school vocabulary.'

Although she has now become a national role model for women of all colours, there is no difference between her public and private faces. 'I don't allow myself to live a double life like most business people do,' she explains. 'If I'm struggling, I'll say so. I don't have to put on an act. When you can be honest, the stress level is far lower. I really believe in the value of the rags-to-riches tale for making people realise that at the end of the day, it's your talent that counts.' She may have learnt the recipes from her Grandmother, but the fighting spirit is all her own.

## Brian Angliss – The Racer

Brooklands (where the A3 meets the M25) is considered by many to be the home of British motor racing and the birthplace of aviation. As early as 1909, cars raced around its banked circuit, and in 1908 A.V. Roe made the first flight in a British-built aeroplane from the grass airstrip. Although the racing circuit closed at the outbreak of the Second World War, its aviation future was assured. Both the Wellington bomber and the Battle of Britain fighter – the Hawker Hurricane – were mass-produced from the Brooklands site.

Today, the racing circuit is broken and covered in weeds and the aerodrome is an industrial estate. High-performance engines can still be heard but they are not ghostly echoes of the circuit's illustrious past. They emanate from the new 90,000 square foot factory premises of AC Cars and Autokraft Limited.

Brian Angliss is managing director and a major shareholder in the two companies. His company builds one of the fastest and most highly finished British sports cars ever made – the AC Cobra. 'AC Cars have been making racing cars since 1901,' says Angliss, 'and we have a safe full of all the trophies they have won here at Brooklands over the years.'

Angliss has a fascination for large petrol engines. Walking round his factory, guests are treated to the spectacle of a great British sports car being lovingly built by craftsmen. Then they can see hundreds of classic motorbikes in pristine condition. There are also a few vintage cars. (Angliss likes to keep his staff motivated and interested so he rotates them from project to project every so often.) The factory is a breathtaking site, because apart from the cars and motorbikes there is a Second World War fighter aeroplane – a Hawker Hurricane. This has a 54-litre, 3,000 horsepower engine. But for impact nothing can beat the ex-army Gazelle helicopter complete with fire control systems that Angliss travels to work in.

'Very few people, myself included, go to work just for the sheer pleasure of working. We all have to work to earn money to live. The aeroplanes, sports cars and motorbikes all add interest to the business. Not just for myself but for the staff too. Anything that helps you get out of bed in the morning, can't be all bad.'

Angliss shrugs off admiration: 'It's just work to me. Producing high-quality cars is a serious business. The aeroplanes and motorbikes add a little spice,' he says modestly.

Angliss employs 60 craftsmen in producing the Cobra. Every aspect of the car is hand-built and finished. There are 2,000 man hours put into each one. The upholstery is cut from leather hides and is hand-stitched. The aluminium body panels are beaten out of sheet by hand. With 18 coats of paint and a tuned 5.0-litre engine, the cars will go from 0 to 60 mph in under five seconds.

'I'm no car enthusiast,' says Angliss, 'cars for me are a business and nothing more. If it was any other way, I would have gone broke long ago.' He says that in the early days the cars were a hobby, 'but the glitter soon wears off when your hobby becomes a cold business and the bank manager is breathing down your neck.'

Although he is unromantic about his job, he does get tremendous satisfaction and pride from the product. 'It is a feeling that runs throughout the company, from the youngster fresh from school to the semi-retired panel beater. Each person in the company has a job to do and no one allows their department to be the one that falls behind in standards of workmanship. Craftsmen who can create something with just the skill in their hands are becoming scarce. Here, skilled people are amongst other skilled people, they respect each other through their skills even though they may be of different trades.'

One thing Angliss is emphatic about is respect. 'We have had managers who have had the authority but not the respect.' He remembers saying to one recently promoted employee: 'I can pin a badge on you which says manager, but respect you have to earn.'

It has to be this way because his buyers have the highest standards of all. The majority of them are Japanese. 'They buy a car that is literally a work of art but accept this as the norm. This attitude is spreading to the Western world, and why not...?'

This is all a long way from where he started out. He left school at 16 with a rebuilt motorbike and no qualifications. He became an apprentice toolmaker and then, at the age of 22, after turning his Jaguar upside down, decided that he should be in the car repair business. 'I just looked for the most interesting motor car to get involved with. Thus began my relationship with AC Cars and the Cobra. I was young, foolish and incredibly naive but managed to talk my bank manager into a £100 overdraft, which I hadn't a clue how I was going to repay. Little did I know then that I would be permanently in the red for the next twenty years.'

He started doing an improved copy of the Cobra under licence from AC Cars. By the late 1970s he was exporting these to North America. 'The business just grew and unfortunately my overdraft grew with it. I had fallen into the age-old trap of not wanting anything to do with my paper work. I was a manual worker and that was that. Cash flow forecasts? Never heard of them. My bank manager tried to help me but I always ignored him. Looking back I still shudder when I remember how the business was run. It was all by the seat of my pants with little more than instinct to tell me whether I was doing well or not.'

Unfortunately, his next bank manager was not a car enthusiast and told him one Wednesday that he would not be able to draw the wages on Friday. This happened twice in quick succession and the bank took a charge on his house and business. 'I learnt fast that the life-blood of a business is cash and that it is essential to know precisely at all times the cash position of the company. I can remember even valuing the stationery and coffee cups to convince the auditor we were still alive.'

After several years of struggling he eventually brought the business around. 'It was a fight and we really had to work at it. So many times we thought it was the end then at the last possible moment something would come through. It was like somebody up there playing games with us.'

Angliss had to take a long hard look at what he was trying to do. So far he had only tried to get bigger and produce more cars. 'Part of our problem was that we were concerned with quantity. We were doing eight cars a month. We cut this back to four and concentrated on quality and detail. This halved the costs of stock and work in progress and enabled us to be far more selective on personnel. We decided to increase the price and only make to order. I discovered that big is not necessarily beautiful. We have no plans to expand. We are small enough to duck and dive with the market and take immediate action if necessary. We also have a financial safety net in the bank which gives a nice warm feeling.'

He does not consider his own success to be extraordinary: 'You have to decide what you want. If you want to change things, you just have to make a list and start at the top. Gaining the respect of people is also important – without that you can't do anything.'

He also has a number of personal ground rules he sticks by. He never takes work home and he always works nine to five, although he says: 'Work is a way of life which you cannot help but think about every waking minute.' Some nights he admits to lying awake for hours on end to think through a difficult business strategy. 'I find the brain is uncluttered in the dark silence and presents ideal conditions for thinking.'

His advice to other would-be entrepreneurs is practical: 'If you

## The Unemployables

haven't passed exams, don't worry, the majority wouldn't help you one bit in starting your own business anyway. One might take the view that passing exams is just about remembering what's in a textbook. But give that person a practical application and they're lost. If all the "experts on business" are really that bright, why aren't they millionaires? Education will not teach you how to deal with people. You learn more by doing it yourself. If you are going to study, pick a subject that will be useful to you in business, especially financial subjects.'

His attitude to risk is similar: 'Take chances by all means but not until you are in control. Be prepared to change and adapt to new ideas and situations and make the best of them.'

Angliss also believes people should never be afraid of breaking away from the pack: 'I hate conformity, trying to pretend you're something you're not, and in a conforming world I probably miss a lot of business opportunities. I never wear a suit or a tie to work, it's too uncomfortable. Occasionally for big meetings I do, but only out of respect for the positions of the others attending.'

He also says wryly that there are too many people around who give advice on success who haven't achieved it themselves. 'Try to watch other people and learn by their mistakes to see where they went wrong or right. Listen only to those people who have done it. Too many people will tell you what's what who couldn't even run a bath.'

He still keeps up a wide range of adrenaline-boosting hobbies which include flying, a natural progression from sailing and motorbikes . 'You can't mollycoddle yourself. I think it was Sir Malcolm Campbell who said when you lose your enthusiastic outlook on life, you're dead.'

## The Rise and Fall of John Ashcroft – Whizz-kid

John Ashcroft has done everything quickly in his life so far. He has been quick to make a million, quick to reach the top of the tree and quick to lose it all and fall back down.

Even as a boy, Ashcroft was doing everything faster than everyone else. He was a bright kid. So bright in fact his school put him up for the now defunct Eleven Plus exam at the age of ten. They reckoned without the rules of Upholland Grammar School near Wigan, however, who turned him down because he was too young. So he did his Eleven Plus again to prove it was no fluke (one of the few ever to take it twice) and was duly accepted.

Although Ashcroft came from a relatively poor background he is honest about the mining tradition in his family: 'Please don't get too hung up on this miner's son stuff. After all, my grandfather did own the mine!' Nevertheless money was an important consideration because his teachers had wanted him to go to the better school, Bolton Grammar, but his father said it was too expensive. Everything was financed through the state system and no scholarships were available.

The whizz-kid, however, continued unabated despite the lower-grade school. Ashcroft was fastracked through his education, taking four O levels a year ahead of schedule and three more a year later. The A levels in History, French and Economics followed a bare year after, and he was immediately accepted for the London School of Economics (LSE) in 1966. Again, he was held back for a year, as the school felt he was too young, so he opted to do another A level in General Studies. He eventually went to the LSE in 1967. He attributes much of his success to 'extremely encouraging parents'.

At LSE, and since, he never felt his background was a help or a hindrance and after graduating successfully, he was faced with the job market.

The family mine had escaped nationalisation and had struggled on into the 1960s, but Ashcroft's ambitions lay outside mining: 'I had made up my mind pretty early on that I wanted to go into industry.' On the face of it, he says his education didn't prepare him for anything. There was little correlation between what he learnt and what he later applied. He says this is where he developed his 'jigsaw' mentality of building up a total picture of the company. This emerged in his peculiar management style of segmentation and analysis which was later to become the hallmark of his success. It simply involved breaking business problems down quantitatively and subjecting them to detailed scrutiny in terms of ratios and statistics.

Ashcroft says he was never a great believer in the 'human side' of psychological motivational books or gurus, but he did make it his ambition to acquire knowledge: 'I wanted to learn as much as I could as quickly as I could.' In one of his early jobs at Tube Investments he went to visit as many different industries in the group as possible. Even later as chairman and chief executive of Coloroll this was to continue: 'I always found time to visit at least two different industries or businesses per month.'

By the time he had reached his twenties, Ashcroft had decided what he wanted to do and had set off to do it: 'I can say that there were relatively few events which changed the way I thought. In general, they just increased my determination to stay ahead of the game as much as possible. I would do my job as well and as quickly as I could before moving on to the next opportunity.'

Ashcroft says he never modelled himself on any great managers or motivational heroes. This, however, did not mean he was unwilling to learn from others. Ashcroft's bookshelves at his home are littered with biographies, autobiographies, management and economic textbooks.

In his early career he quickly changed jobs (usually every three years or so) to get further up the tree. He was advancing through the hierarchy at the Reed Paper Group when he spotted the opportunity at Coloroll in 1980. The company was a small wallpaper manufacturer based in Nelson in Lancashire. They needed a managing director who could inject some pace into the company. Resigning from Reed was a risk, but Ashcroft could clearly see the chance: 'There was a definite opportunity in the market at the time. There was not much competition and there was a good manufacturing base.' Ashcroft's first action was to computerise the company's sales and finance departments. He then invested the profits into design to produce a new range of products catering for the rapidly expanding DIY market. The combination of simple, cheap, mass appeal was replicated by many other famous entrepreneurs in this period during in the eighties such as Laura Ashley, Alan Sugar, Richard Branson and others.

As the organisation grew, Ashcroft looked for the big picture, and started to add other companies which had a good corporate 'fit'. Thus pottery and textile companies were added to the group, which just grew larger and larger. By 1987, at 38, he was in charge of one of the largest groups in the UK. Ashcroft had boosted his salary to in excess of £500,000 and had a whole range of executive perks. He was eulogised as one of the most talented young entrepreneurs in the country and moved among senior politicians and society figures. The paragon of success...and then came the recession.

If there was ever a man for whom Rudyard Kipling wrote his poem 'If...', then that man must be John Ashcroft. A few years ago, at the tender age of 40, he was at the top of the tree. He had international renown as being one of Britain's most shrewd and successful entrepreneurs. Then came a year of wrestling with the £350m of debt the company had taken on, plus the after effects of a humiliating resignation.

When the country began to enter the recession in 1989, Coloroll proved extremely vulnerable because its major market was first-time home-buyers, a group hit particularly hard by high interest rates. The revenues dried up, and in June 1990 the company collapsed. Ashcroft was hit by a bout of hepatitis which put him out of circulation for three months: 'When you take the top job, you take the ultimate responsibility. You can't let it go scapegoating down the structure,' he says philosophically. He cut his losses and accepted that there was little he could do to stop the financial haemorrhage that took place: 'The rate at which the business died was really quite frightening, and the final year was just a nightmare.'

Ashcroft says he had seen the whole thing coming as long ago as 1988: 'It was clear there was going to be a down-turn, but I thought it was going to come later, because we were promised a soft landing. When I look back at 1988 there were debts everywhere and we could have ended up in much more serious trouble than we did.' He points out that the main reasons for failure were that he simply didn't have enough time to bring all the acquisitions he had made together. This left him with too much debt in the company from several duplicated overheads: 'When confronted with a storm, you try to make sure everything is rigged, and it wasn't.'

As terrible as the last years were, his faith is completely unshaken: 'It's made me much more relaxed. Now I don't tend to take things so seriously. Experience has taught me to keep things in perspective.'

Ashcroft says one of the most difficult things was that he had created an empire in his own image and that it was therefore difficult to take the knife to it: 'Towards the end it desperately needed stronger management and that was at a time when I was being criticised for being autocratic. I couldn't win either way. The thing is when you're in a company that is growing rapidly you can make a mistake every week and it won't matter because the business is expanding rapidly. It's only when it turns down that the mistakes begin to show. When that happens each mistake hits you full in the face. You're able to take so much more in your stride when the business is going well.'

He says the press were particularly spiteful: 'I never complained – you have to learn quickly how the system works but there are still a couple of journalists I won't talk to. The good thing is that nobody can ever write something about me now which is going to hurt me. I don't care anymore.'

Although many said he was a ruthless autocrat, Ashcroft believes his success was very much due to the success he had managing people: 'I always liked to give them their own authority. You can "smell" a good business. I look at people's basic skills and see how they can best be utilised. One thing I never did was to get rid of all the old staff, because you lose so much in terms of contacts and experience.'

If people want to do well in a company then Ashcroft's message is straightforward: 'If you are given a job, get it done ahead of schedule and do it well.' He says experience is important in a particular field, and personality is more so, but: '... you have to realise that different people have different styles – they may be quiet or extrovert but they can still have the same ability.'

He says he always looked for the best in his people, which is a particular feature of his thinking now: 'When you hit a bad patch you never know if you'll come out, but you have to believe in yourself. You have to find a positive aspect to everything and concentrate on your strengths. You don't have to be clever to succeed in business, you just have to be lucky and in the right place. It's interesting from my point of view, because I never really knew whether Coloroll was a fluke.'

'My ambition now is just to run a business and make it grow. The money is a by-product.'

What lessons has he learnt? 'It's important to be personally relaxed about business. Sometimes your train goes off the rails and you just have to make a massive effort to lift it back on.' There's no doubt that under the affable exterior Ashcroft is still sensitive about what happened, but he is typically bullish. He says the most important tips for success are to '...trust your own judgements. Don't necessarily be swayed by what people say. Only listen to wise counsellors and they are rare. A lot of successful people run out of personal capacity to do more, because they don't have enough good people to help them.'

The whizz-kid may finally have slowed down, but only to pause for reflection: 'There are no regrets. The good side was that I was able to pack a lot into a short period of time. My motivations certainly are still towards growth and progress, but some of my friends who are still in business think it has been a little like the tortoise and the hare,' he says laughing.

## Douglas Bader – Hero and Villain

If proof was ever needed that man thrives on challenge, Douglas Bader is it. His achievements are well documented in book and film, but what is less well known is what his character was like.

One thing was certain: the pugnacious Bader, although popular, was not universally liked, but then again that is not a requirement for success. His colleagues argued with him over tactics and some people simply could not get on with him. The essential truth was that there was a demon in Bader, for good and ill.

He was born in 1910 and joined the RAF as an officer cadet. He was amongst the best of his group and excelled at sport and low-level aerobatics. Even then he was headstrong and apt to be overconfident. One day in 1931 some pilots were teasing him about his ability to do stunts. Typically, he set out to prove a point but ended up crashing and nearly killing himself.

Although he lost both his legs he soon got a pair of artificial ones. Colleagues remember him at the time as being particularly stubborn about not using a stick. Time after time he fell, and time after time he got back up again. He used to do this so much in the early days that some people thought he was obsessed and couldn't see reason. He fought tooth and nail with his disability and refused to give in. The side of his character people said was overbearing, dogmatic and pig-headed was the same side that spurred him on to overcome his difficulties. Bader had to be unreasonable about his life because it had been so unreasonable towards him.

To some, he seemed a man with a chip on his shoulder, constantly trying to prove a point. No doubt there was some bitterness in him. He lost his legs on the eve of being selected to play rugby for England, one of his greatest ambitions. He was tormented by nightmares in which he would have his legs and wake up to find them gone. One of his girlfriends at the time of the crash was packed off to South Africa by a mother frightened of her falling in love with a cripple. No doubt all these things took their toll on him.

Not only did Bader have to get used to being disabled, but he also was invalided out of the air force. This was particularly frustrating for him because he was quite capable of flying, but RAF regulations did not cover his case so he could not gain a pilot's rating for his circumstances. This showed another part of Bader's character – he was mentally strong. Overcoming physical pain was as great a challenge for him as the emotional strain of being out of the RAF.

From 1932 until 1939 he was a civilian and had no service rank, no privileges and not much money. This was in a time before the National Health Service, when men disabled by war selling bootlaces to make a living were a common sight on the streets of London. Bader may be known for his wartime exploits, but this was the hardest time for him.

As soon as it was clear that war would break out Bader applied again to the RAF. Again they said he was perfectly able to fly but couldn't pass him. This time Bader didn't give in and used every bit of influence he had. Due to a shortage of pilots he was allowed in. All of his colleagues from the early thirties had gained rank when Bader came back and he felt quite old at thirty being a simple pilot officer. But he was soon taking out his aggression on the German air force as the leader of his own squadron.

The outfit he was sent to command had a morale problem. The pilots thought that a legless commanding officer was going to be the last straw. Bader seemed to realise this immediately, and one of the first things he did was to show how he could handle an aeroplane. For half an hour he pulled out every trick in the book, again to prove a point. His men quickly came to respect him and he became a legend throughout Fighter Command and the RAF.

One of the facts not widely known about Bader was that he was probably a better fighter pilot because of his disabilities. He had no extremities for blood to drain to, so when other pilots were blacking out in violent manoeuvres, he was still alert. Another fact was that when he baled out, had it not been for his artificial leg coming off, he would have been dragged down to his death.

The young and inexperienced pilots who flew with Bader said they all felt quite invulnerable when he was around, because he was such an inspirational character. They also said, however, that he expected them to live up to his own standards, which was difficult for anybody.

During this period he became a larger-than-life character and was in his element swashbuckling around with his team. He was fiercely loyal to them all and took anybody's death personally. He also turned a blind eye to the rules and freely chatted to ground controllers about golf and squash, anything which could help calm the nerves of his young pilots. He even used to smoke his pipe in the cockpit on the way back from missions, something strictly against the regulations for fear of fire.

## The Unemployables

For a long time everyone thought Bader had a charmed life, but he eventually crashed in France one day after a collision with another aeroplane and was captured. He escaped immediately, but was recaptured, and as he was thought to be a difficult man to handle he was sent to Colditz castle, where escape was supposed to be impossible. In 1945 he was eventually liberated from there, and despite his efforts to get back into the war it was all over before he got the chance.

After the war, Shell, for whom he had worked in the thirties, offered him his old job back, and even gave him his own aeroplane to fly round the world on aviation business. Bader spent many years working with various charities for the disabled and went out of his way to write to children who had been disabled. He became a scratch golfer and used to amaze people with how well he could drive a golf ball.

There is no doubt that luck provided many opportunities in Bader's life, but part of his strength was the way he optimised every chance.

There were some people who disliked Bader. They saw a different side of the character which was built up to be a legend. His achievement still stands as testimony to human achievement although Colin Hodgkinson, a lesser-known contemporary of Bader's, lost both his legs even before he learned to fly.

Paul Brickhill, Bader's biographer, summarised his life by quoting Shakespeare: 'There's nothing either good or bad but thinking makes it so.' This applies as much to Bader's life as to people's opinion of him.

## Andy Brown – The Student Entrepreneur

There can be few places worse than Crawley town centre in the rain. Its concrete slabs are streaked with the dark stains of acid rain which pours over the sides of the tower blocks into the square below. People hustle by and woe betide anyone who tries to stop them to ask questions about their favourite products. It is a depressing and soul-destroying place, but it's the place where Andy Brown laid the foundations of his marketing business when he was twenty-four.

Even at that young age, he was no stranger to the great outdoors. He been running a gardening business since he was fourteen and he left school to concentrate on it. After two years of shovelling muck, he decided that he should continue his education and learn more about business. The local polytechnic was five times oversubscribed for the business studies course he wanted to do. He still managed to talk his way onto it, on the basis that he was an active businessman and would learn more than the other students.

As soon as he came out of college he set up his company Insight, offering market research services. This meant going around with a clipboard asking people questions about a product. 'It was hard work, but it had to be done. I still do it these days if I want to ensure the job's done properly. It didn't make much money, but I survived,' he says. Now his business has grown into a full service marketing consultancy.

'It's very important to keep overheads down,' says Brown emphatically, 'manage the process profitably and bring everything in on a needs basis. When we pitch against other agencies we don't have a flash office to support, so we can provide better value for money. We don't have a lot of staff.' (Brown has four staff – himself, two account planners and a production controller). 'I simply said to people, "I don't have much experience but I'm cheap." It's one of the great misunderstandings of business; you don't need experience at all, you need enthusiasm and initiative. You can learn the rest or get others to do it for you. You must have discipline, though and you must be prepared to work hard.'

Brown says all he does is to get inside the client's mind: 'You need to know what he's trying to achieve.' For instance, he always uses the client's product and watches how it is sold. He finds out everything about the way the company works. Only then does he make his recommendations. He sometimes takes this to ridiculous extremes: 'A while ago, I did 400 hundred interviews on the streets to research Hawaiian Tropic sun tan lotion. It actually enabled me to go back to the research company J. Walter Thompson (a top London agency) and talk authoritatively on what the man in the street thought about the product.'

Brown admits that standing in the street interviewing people is an awful job: 'People run away from you, swear at you or just and try and avoid you, but it tells you what you need to know about the product.'

Encouraged by his success with the major advertising agencies, he decided to start his own. Brown believes in hiring top-class talent so he encouraged a 45-year-old partner who used to work for another top advertising agency, Saatchi and Saatchi, to join the company.

'You have to work with people you like,' says Brown. 'If I don't like them, client or employee, I decide not to do business with them anymore. There's no point working with people who don't appreciate you. It's rare and it's really an admission of defeat. I don't like people getting one up on me.'

The strategy seems to be working. Insight is regularly beating the largest London-based agencies for work. Recently he won the account of Southern Water, one of the biggest companies in the South. This currently represents 80 per cent of his business. He won the account because he was fast enough to react when the company put him on the pitch list four days before the account review.

Why does he think he's been so successful? 'Because I've been prepared to do things other people don't want to do. The problem is people see business as being dirty somehow. Some people think it's better to be a clerk and earn a decent wage than it is to sell things and make a lot of money.'

'A lot of my friends went to work in big companies, but they don't have much effect on the way the company works. When I was working in a big company I was always bumping into the regulations. I found it depressing. I wasn't a maverick, I just didn't want other people to take credit for what I'd done. There were just too many levels to get through. Now there's only me that stands between success and failure.'

Brown had to put up with his college friends having company cars for several years. 'I never had a problem with people who had flash cars or executive brief cases, because they weren't free and it wasn't their car. Besides I wanted my money to be in the business not parked outside it.'

Did he ever consider going into business as being a risk? 'What are you risking? Running up the student overdraft further? Not having a car? Not having a lifestyle? I'd been a student for four years. I didn't know what a lifestyle was!' Although he is now much better off, he still retains his 'student' views: 'I'm not political, but I am vegetarian and I do recycle things. There are also clients I won't work with, like tobacco companies and car companies that use sex to advertise.'

If there's one thing he wants to avoid, it's going into public relations.

'Public relations always reminds me of fat opera singers and I hate it, and parties with lots of thing on sticks. They call themselves "people people" and it couldn't be further from the sort of professional consultants we are,' he says.

On the rare occasions when Brown is not working, he is reading. He reads everything, soaking up every last piece of knowledge: 'It's no substitute for experience, but it helps.'

Although Brown was in business before he went to college he says there is little he can do now that he couldn't before: 'It just served to give me more confidence, and it was also good fun, but it wasn't absolutely essential.'

Brown's advice to those who want to set up on their own is: 'Do it. If you fail or if you succeed, you will learn something and that's the essential thing. If you do nothing, you'll learn nothing.' Brown feels that it's not important to be wildly successful, but it is important to try. If people do that then they have scored at least one victory. All they need then is to string the victories together and they become a success.

## Linda Beard – Designs on Success

In a beautiful flat overlooking London's Regent's Park, Linda Beard sits and works. The place, it has to be said, is magnificent. It is not difficult to guess what she does by the decor of her home. Beard is a designer and her wallcoverings made Coloroll, the home furnishings group, a household name. She would come up with the designs and John Ashcroft's brilliant business skills would sell them.

She started out, however, a long way from the manicured lawns of Regent's Park. Beard is from Wallasey, near Liverpool and she went to art college there and set up on her own as a freelance designer. 'A few people came to see me and I was getting quite a bit of interest, but in those days I couldn't afford to live in London so I used to work at my parents' house in Liverpool. At first I thought the whole idea of industrial design was really boring; most designers make the mistake of thinking that.'

She says the North was fairly dour in those days, but 'the sense of humour was fabulous. The Liverpool wit is brilliant'. Just as well really – there wasn't much up North to laugh about then. 'At that time you could go around firms in Manchester where the boss would come up and say "we tek students and lahk to train thum ower way. We dun't nid fresh ahdeas here".' Beard says one of the problems with companies at the time was that they were content to stand still and not develop. It was Beard's sheer enthusiasm that penetrated this attitude.

There is no obvious clue as to why Beard should be so motivated. Neither of her parents were particularly ambitious, although Beard herself had started off in life wanting to be a ballerina. 'But my parents couldn't afford that, so I went into design. Now I still love to go to the ballet, but it is just an interest.'

She is still not sure how it all happened: 'I really went to art school because I couldn't work out what I wanted to do. I never wanted to be better than anyone else, I just wanted to do things the best I could in whatever way. I'll often work all night to get something finished, because I feel so personally about it. I wouldn't say it's necessarily a good thing to be. But it's a bit like writing; I can identify with great artists – I get tremendous highs and lows. I get a terrific rush at times and then go through the floor. If you're quite successful you can sometimes start to hate the business of designing because of the ups and downs you get.'

Whatever the problem, she would not swap it because it allows her to excel at her particular art: 'If I'd been a ballerina, I could never have put up with being a second swan, I would have wanted to be the best. That's still the way I feel. I try and bring a theatrical element into what I do to fire people with enthusiasm. The good thing about being a northerner is that I do have this down-to-earth streak in me. Don't mistake the trappings of wealth for security, I still get very upset if people criticise my work.'

Beard says she never coveted wealth or possessions, but just seems to have been lucky. Her message is simple: work out what you like doing, do it, and you will do it well, become good at it and be successful. 'The funny thing was that I used to do all this when I was a child and now I get paid for it, but it's part of me and it always has been. Sometimes I hate it but I soon get to like it again. I'm not an artist – I'm an industrial artist – there is a difference. I have to be a lot more practical. If I have a good idea it has to sell – I can never be too careful in what I do. I have to take some risks because it is expected from a progressive designer.'

She ascribes much of her success to learning more about the way business is done: 'I don't know what it is that makes one person buy something and not another – the whole process of business fascinates me. I love to meet the people on the shop floor who work with the designs. I learned a lot about business from John Bray (one of the brains behind Coloroll), and that helped me. Let's face it, there's no point doing something unless you can make a living at it, so I had to know something about business.'

What Beard did next was what anyone could do. She worked out what people might want and touted her ideas around: 'I came up with the idea of coordinated designs linking wallcoverings with bedding and curtains, etc., and I took them to Coloroll. That's when the company started to take off. The coordinate range really became popular and they all had my name on them. Then I was working with them right the way through until they went bust.'

She is very careful about attention to detail: 'At first I did everything: I did the design, the colouring, stood over the machine, did the pattern book layout and I used to go to the screen printers. I could never get off that wheel of involvement. Now I have one or two people to work for me doing all that sort of stuff.'

But she is still heavily involved. The hallmark of her work is massive enthusiasm and boundless energy: 'You should be prepared to sell your ideas. It's not enough to have good ideas, you have to go out and sell them. We have some of the best designers in this country and they all seem to go abroad, but there are big opportunities here. You just have to go out there and talk to companies and listen to what they want. You must always be prepared to stop and think again. There are so many talented people out there who really look down on working in business. They all want to be fashion designers.

Sometimes I go into companies and I want to shake people and give them some enthusiasm for what they do. A lot of successful people do that – John Ashcroft from Coloroll was very good at shaking things up and introducing new ideas.'

If there's one thing she stresses, it's injecting energy into what she does: 'You've got to have get up and go, and understand what people want. Design can be a really lonely thing because only you can do it, but it's very gregarious talking to people to find out what they want.'

Whatever the pitfalls of the profession, it has paid dividends for Beard. She has a flat in London and a house in Cornwall, which is her second home, but: 'I'm not into flash cars or anything like that. But I do like music and walking in the countryside with my dog. In fact my dog's more of a success than me. I found him in Lancashire. Now that's a real rags to riches story!'

## Will Carling – Playing to Win

The essence of success according to Will Carling is to treat your challenges as a sportsman treats his game. Relax, enjoy it and naturally you will succeed.

Carling has taken this one stage further than just applying it to his captaincy of one of England's most successful rugby union teams; he has formed a company together with Mike Brearley, Tony Jacklin, Gary Lineker, Adrian Moorhouse and management brain, Jim Foley. The company, called Insights, helps business people benefit from the leadership skills of great sportsmen.

'Most successful people show the same principles of leadership that you see in the greatest sportsmen,' says Jim Foley. 'A lot of the time they don't realise that they are following some of the most widely laid down principles that are taught in the world's most prestigious business schools.'

It works both ways. 'Many people in business apply some of the sportsman's greatest abilities, without even knowing it,' he adds. 'They develop the people around them, they think out strategies, they develop their own skills.'

Insights gets business people away on residential courses where they can look closely at the strengths and weaknesses they have. 'Self-analysis is essential. You can't begin to improve yourself unless you know where to direct the effort. We all tend to underplay ourselves and not take ourselves seriously. That's the problem with many people. They just have a really low self-esteem. It's not just people in the street. It applies all the way up to senior management. If you don't value yourself, then no one else will. If you want to be successful – in anything – you have to start believing that you can do it and in time you will.'

It is clear why these big sports names put their trust in Foley. He recognised the link between what they did and what goes on in business and was articulate and clever enough to bring the two together. As much as Insights is about applying sports leadership in business, it is testimony to Foley's ability and drive to create an organisation which helps people realise their full potential: 'We owe it to ourselves to get people to realise their full potential.' Perhaps that can be described as the way to become truly successful – help others. If you really can help others, whether it be in business or any walk of life, you will be successful. There is a saying that the giver is always the receiver and nowhere is this truer than in sport.

Foley is as enthusiastic about Insights as he is about every other aspect of life. If he wasn't in business he's the sort of chap that National Power would connect up to the National Grid. What Foley has realised is that there is a huge market for self-improvement. What better way to make a living than by helping others?

'So many of us don't have the confidence to follow our own instincts, and this is the theory behind our business – that these concepts don't have to be put over in a stuffy way. When you listen to Tony Jacklin you can identify with him. To follow your instincts is natural, yet so few of us have the confidence. We have this marvellous piece of equipment – the human brain – that most of us fail to use to its full ability.'

One of the courses that Foley devised was for Tony Jacklin to teach business people how to create teams out of 'prima donnas'. When Jacklin brought the Ryder cup team together he had to take a group of individuals and make them into a team – exactly what successful people do every day of the week in business.

Typically the sort of clients that Insights has are chief executives and senior business people. The principle that Foley has latched onto, however, is something that can be applied at every level, not just to great national sporting celebrities: it can be recognised in sportsmen kicking a ball around in the local park. Enjoy yourself, set an example for people to follow, encourage others, be pleased with success, and determined by failure. Everyday these examples can be seen all over the world.

'Sometimes it's difficult to get senior people to take self-improvements seriously, because they don't think they need it. This is the same at every level of life. Those who most need self-improvement are least aware of it. Recognising the need for it is half the battle. Some business people say it's all very well for sports people because they don't know what it's like under pressure, but Carling, Jacklin, Moorhouse and Lineker have all done it in full view of the world. They have the credibility to stand in front of business people because they have experienced all the pressures.'

Foley and Will Carling are branches off the same vine: 'I don't know whether you ever really discover that you have a talent for leading people. I just found that I'd been playing in teams from the age of seven and I preferred to be in a position where I could say something rather than being led and it just went on from there. It's not something I got from the family,' says Carling.

Carling's father was in the army and was a good man-manager, 'but it's really not up to me to say whether I'm a good leader. I always wanted to play for England. I thought if I'm honest that's what I want to do. I didn't just want to play for England. I knew that I wanted to be in a successful England team.'

Carling was made Captain at the age of 22, the youngest-ever England Captain. It was difficult coming into a team where people had four or five years' experience as internationals: 'The only thing I could do was to be honest and say, "Look, you all know a lot more about this than I do." I just had to get everyone to contribute their views. So we involved everybody on the training procedures and over time we just grew together.'

Carling is quite clear about his success formula: 'The key to success is preparation. I want to be part of the best team in the world. What you say to people on the pitch is not as important as everything you do before you get onto it. The image is made before the game.'

His style is leadership from the front: 'You have to do everything you can to make the team successful. The team is more important to me than anything else. If I ever felt I was not doing a good enough job, I would pack it in. I will train as hard as I can to make the team successful and I expect everyone else to do the same.' When they're losing, tired and under pressure he will 'ask them how much they wanted to win. You have to call on thoughts and emotions that will make them less tired and give their all.'

Carling says that details make people successful: 'Sometimes it's just little things; you've always got to be on time for training sessions, you've got to listen. It's easy to fool around. You have to have honesty and integrity. Because if someone's late and you try and crack the whip, they will not respect you. I want to win and I want to be part of this team, so I will set the example.'

The most important qualities are: 'Honesty. Honesty with yourself and with others. Loyalty, and that's not misplaced loyalty – if someone's not good enough then you tell them. And preparation is the other. You must visualise everything first. Think it all through in your head. Create your own personal game plan. In something like rugby and football, to have respect you have to play well. If my standard goes I would be dropped. It's vital to get yourself right if you want to get the best from the team.'

Why is Carling so driven? What is it that makes him want to win? 'I can't honestly see the reason for doing something unless you want to be the best at it. Otherwise what's the point? Things have got to be a challenge. You've got to be honest with yourself. Sometimes you're not going to be the best, but you can always improve. You know where you can get to – so get there. Make an honest assessment of what your potential is, and that applies in sport, in business, in life, in general. Make no excuses and go for it! You've got to go for the maximum otherwise you're never going to be satisfied.'

How is he going to communicate this to others? 'If you sit down and talk to the Jacklins and Brearleys, you will see that they have known the pain of fear of failure and they've got up and gone again and you can respect that. There are too many people who are too frightened of failure even to try being successful so they tone down their ambitions. So many people can achieve what they want. So many will achieve what they want. They have real potential but never realise it.'

Carling says he admires people like Daly Thompson: 'I'm privileged enough to spend some time with him and he's such an inspirational leader. You get a real buzz off people like that.'

What will he be challenged by after rugby? 'Well, I don't feel as if I'm at the top of my form yet. The minute I think I'm at the top, then I'll pack it in. Of course it's nice when you win. You take a real sense of satisfaction; you must aim for perfection because you know you'll never get there, but you know you have to keep trying. I know at the back of my mind that I'm lucky to be where I am. I have a lot of fun.'

The worst thing about it all, according to Carling, is the media attention: 'They tend to either set you up as the best or the worst. Of course it's their job to sell papers, but sometimes they can be annoying. But when the pressure's on you must believe in what you're doing. You can't give in to what people say. You must stick by your beliefs. We all know how we played, and I know whether I've played well or not. I don't need telling.'

Carling gets very involved in the selection of players. They have to believe they've got the real potential for international rugby: 'They've got to have the right mental make-up to add to the team. The right attitude is essential; if they're the best player in the world and they've got a bad attitude they won't be selected. They also have to want to be part of the team because rugby is a team game. It's not just about scoring tries – they have to want to play for the team.'

Obviously playing at international level is highly pressurised and he tries to help players by keeping the squad light-hearted: 'Humour is essential – if the team thinks a character is strong he will get a nickname and he will get ribbed. If he's not a strong character they will leave him alone to develop at his own pace. Sometimes I will talk to a player who's nervous and say to him, "I've seen you play in this situation against so-and-so and you were brilliant. Think about how you did that day. I know you can succeed here today." You have to get them into the positive frame of mind. It only takes a few words. Just tell them how good they are. Having said that, I can't get into someone's mind; all I can do is to create the environment in which they can motivate themselves. If someone's negative, it's difficult to get them out. You have to visualise success. We use a lot of video clips, so that people can actually see what they're doing.'

Despite the pressures, Carling is obviously enjoying himself. In different ways he and Jim Foley are men at the top of their form, yet still wanting to do better. The hallmark of classic sportsmen. The message is clear: if you want success you have to play to win.

## Bob Champion – Unassuming Hero

You get used to achievers who are the get-up-and-go, take-the-world-by-the-scruff-of-the-neck types. They're the sort of people who are obvious, identifiable achievers. But this is not always the case. An exception that proves the rule is Bob Champion. He is a quiet, modest, almost a shy man. Somebody you might not even notice. And that's the way he likes it. He is the typical British hero. Understated, calm, likable. He hates fuss – the sort of chap that would step up to give the enemy a bloody nose and still be back in time for tea and tiffin.

Successful people are usually notable for having achieved at least one major objective in their life. Again, in this respect Bob Champion is different. After conquering the ultimate challenge, his fight against cancer, he went on to win the Grand National. He has since set up the Bob Champion Cancer Trust, had a movie made about him and publicised it around the world, written a book, and now devotes his time to raising money for the Trust and training horses. It's an understatement to say that he is going to be remembered for a lot of things, not just riding horses.

It's been over ten years since his win at the Grand National and he is still at the gallop, attending numerous charity events around the country. By now, after hundreds of interviews, he is used to the media attention and accepts that his fame has cost him his privacy: 'My life was my own before I won the National, but it hasn't been ever since.' This is partly due to the fact that he spends hundreds of hours a year on motorways tavelling to attend the charity bashes.

Despite his many racing successes, Champion is an unassuming man. He describes his achievements as a series of consequences: the establishment of the Bob Champion Cancer Trust was a result of the money that poured in after he won the Grand National and he won the National because he was riding a winner. As simple as that.

But behind the humble, quiet exterior, the desire to win has always been there: 'I wanted to win the National from a very early age. I was always determined when I was a kid, especially when it came to riding horses and ponies. I've always been a little bit stubborn.' Describing himself as a little stubborn is a bit like saying Ghengis Khan liked to travel.

Although he was not dependent on his parents for very long he says that his father's strong character had an influence on his life but he never pushed him to ride. By the time Champion was fifteen, he had left home to work on his uncle's farm and go to college.

In his early years, Champion won show-jumping and horse trials, which inspired him to continue riding. By the time he was thirty he was rated as one of Britain's top jockeys. But his career suddenly came to a halt when he was diagnosed as having cancer. Within a day the doctors operated.

'Cancer is like the will to win. It exists in everybody, you just have to trigger it off. I didn't want to die – I made that decision from the beginning. When I started my treatment I had no doubt in my mind about getting better and I kept giving myself goals.'

At the time when he was struck by cancer, recoveries were rare.

'As soon as the doctor realised that I was in racing she started giving me odds which made me more determined. She said I had a fifty-fifty chance of a full recovery. I don't know what I'd have done if she said I had a fifty to one against chance of living.'

During the few months that followed his operation, he endured a living hell while undergoing chemotherapy treatment, yet within five months of completing it he returned to riding. 'It was more demoralising than anything. The drugs weren't working properly and I was having trouble breathing, especially when I was riding on a cold morning. I was trying to do too much.'

Champion went for six months to race in America, where there wasn't the pressure from home. On his return to Britain, Champion raced – and won – the Grand National. It was the peak in his career as a jockey. 'I was second favourite that day; I could feel the personal support behind me – it willed me over first.'

Champion believes that when you are winning everything starts to go well. It becomes like a habit you get into: 'When a jockey is riding winners, everything goes right because you feel more confident.' After riding over 400 winners in his career, he is speaking from experience. As much as Champion believes that a lot of luck was involved, he admits, for the record, that winning involves some skill.

Those two years read like a fairy-tale come true. But after achieving this, where do you go from there? What else is there to conquer? 'The recession,' Champion says. 'It's the biggest challenge of my life.'

He believes that people can do anything as long as they have their health. He sees people benefiting from the Bob Champion Cancer Trust and, after being close to death, it isn't surprising that his health means everything. He has taken the worst period in his life and turned it around to help other sufferers, many of them children. He has also taken the most successful day in his life and career and used his experience to train 'winners'. It's impossible not to feel inspired by his charity and his life.

The basic problem with human beings is that they all look roughly alike. Same number of limbs, eyes, noses, etc. They're even the same basic shape. Bob Champion shows this can be very deceptive. They all may have the same wrapper, but some have very different centres.

## Shirley Conran – Superwoman

There is a family joke that author Shirley Conran is rather pleased with. It goes: Q. What's the difference between a rottweiler and Shirley Conran?
A. In the end the rottweiler lets go.

'Most of my books are about self-confidence, although I'm quite short of it myself. I'm a tryer and a survivor, though,' she says. She has made millions out of telling people how to get what they want. 'Self-confidence is the most important thing, and this comes from identifying your goals, knowing your limits and roping in all the help you can get.'

Making life work for you rather than vice versa, is what Shirley Conran is all about. Her book, *Down with Superwoman*, was aimed at getting women to realise their full potential by freeing up the amount of time they have for enjoying themselves or pursuing their own activities. This was especially aimed at the nineties' working mother.

Although she is now very well-off and has luxury homes in Provence and Monte Carlo, it hasn't always been so. She started out comfortably enough. She was educated at St. Paul's Girls School in London, where she says, she was first exposed to the idea of making every second count. Then she was sent to finishing school in Switzerland, where she was taught to waste time idly painting and sculpting: 'Up until then I led a sheltered life, because I'd just been brought up to marry a rich man.'

And marry one she did – Terence Conran (later Sir Terence) – but this was doomed to failure. 'I was working with my husband and when we split he fired me from his company. He instructed the accountant to give me a buff envelope which contained four weeks' pay – a total of £48. This was in lieu of a month's notice. So I was left with £48 and two children to look after. This was in 1962 when it wasn't very trendy to be a single-parent family.'

At the time she was living in a basement in London's Camden Town in what she describes as an 'impoverished state'. This was a difficult time for her. She remembers her son Jasper phoning up saying he was having some dental trouble and there was nothing she could do about it: 'He just had to suffer because I couldn't afford to pay the bills. I felt impotent and humiliated.'

## The Unemployables

The divorce was a rude awakening for her. But she took stock of the situation and decided she had to get on with her life: 'I was motivated mainly by the fact I had to earn some money to feed my children.'

Her immediate reaction was to start writing about design. She had been writing design articles for the *Daily Mail* and decided to apply for the job of Home Editor. There were more than 100 applicants for the job, and she got the post because 'I was lucky'.

She enjoyed writing but had to work hard at it to make up for her lack of journalistic experience: 'Just because you are capable of writing, doesn't mean you can be a writer any more than someone saying they want to become an accountant because they can do arithmetic. You can't just do it overnight, you have to really study it and train.'

This attitude paid off and she went on to become the first women's page editor in Fleet Street. But disaster was lurking around the corner again, when in 1970 she fell ill with pneumonia and developed PVS (Post-Viral Syndrome), which laid her low for many months. This gave her a chance to contemplate other ideas.

It was during this period that she met an editor at Sidgwick and Jackson who advised her to write a book about some pet subjects she'd always talked about, i.e. saving time with housework and self-realisation. 'This was mainly because I couldn't afford anyone to do mine, and I hated it so much I wanted to minimise the time I spent doing it.' The book she wrote, *Superwoman,* was eventually published in 1975 and was in the best-seller lists for 19 weeks. She got 20,000 letters in the first fortnight: 'I was terrified by the responsibility. It altered my life in a horrifying way. I got letters saying it had saved marriages and stopped suicides.'

The book told housewives how best to cope with the daily chores – for instance, not to call them 'housework' but 'system-support work', because it would sound more fun to men. She advised women to confront their families as a group and schedule them specific tasks to do. For instance, she advocated asking children with help to look after pets; if they refused, she suggested giving them away (the pets, not the kids).

She developed the book assiduously and even took out advertisements in the personal columns of national newspapers asking readers of her book to write and tell her why they found it useful.

She claims never to have made any real money out of *Superwoman* because she had it rewritten for the woman of every country it was published in. The research costs of this offset any profits that the book made. However, seven years later real wealth came her way when she penned *Lace,* a 'bodice-ripping' romance. Another best-seller, *Lace* was the first in a succession of other novels. They now sell in New York for around $4.75m plus $1.5m for movie rights and these have made her rich: 'I think it's very nice having money now, but I didn't have it when I really needed it.'

This pushed her into the world of famous authors, but it has not cooled her ardour for writing. When she is working she leads a 'nun-like' existence with her two secretaries and her socialising tends to be with other best-selling authors, like Barbara Taylor-Bradford, 'because we have so much in common'. She also believes in keeping fit, but because she is an obsessive worker, she has a trainer come to her: 'If you work all day sitting at a desk you have to ensure that you keep fit. It's something I don't consider to be a luxury.' The exercise takes the form of yoga and occasional swimming disciplines. 'I don't know any other best-seller writers who have time for any hobbies. I like to travel and walk in the foothills of the Himalayas, but I can't imagine having free time.'

The irony is that while being very good at advising others, Conran has never had a settled family life. Since Terence Conran she has married and divorced two more husbands: 'Twice is a coincidence, three times is a pattern.' She says that she is not successful in marriage because she had a very dominant father and that she reacts to a husband like her father. 'It's difficult to get over early conditioning, but you can step over puddles instead of marching through them. I don't intend to have a fourth puddle. Our generation was very much the one that sorted things out. We were pioneers of our emotions.' She says she has been much better at solving other people's problems rather than her own: 'Like a lot of women I'm not very good at being objective.'

She says she enjoys life on her own and has no other ambition than to continue writing and 'be a good grandmother. My attitude is that, basically you should have as good a life as possible and enjoy it as much as you can, and if you don't manage to get something done, put it off until Monday. If you can't do it then, put it off until the next Monday.'

This is clearly the absolute opposite of the way she lives her life and the amount of work she puts into research on a daily basis. Because she writes so much about avoiding housework, she spends quite a bit of her time actually doing it to ensure she remains well-informed: 'I must be the only multi-millionairess who actually washes her own floors.'

## Keith Chorlton – The Right Stuff

It costs nothing. You can't buy it. You can't sell it. But it will make you a happy and wealthy person. What is this thing that will transform your life? Simple. All you need is the right attitude.

So how do you go about getting it? Well, firstly, you can start by talking to Keith Chorlton. Here is a man with no formal education (he claims he couldn't read or write when he left school) and no rich contacts or family background to help him. He comes from a poor South Wales mining background. But now he drives around in a large car with beautiful bodywork. The women he has around him, it has to be said, are something similar.

If you can imagine a cross between Tom Jones and Richard Branson, then Chorlton is it. He is a big burly character with a voice like a gravel and a manner reminiscent of Rocky I, II, III, etc. This is a man whose parents gave him nothing, whose education gave him less, whose brother was murdered, whose life, in short, has not been a bowl of cherries.

Why, and how has he succeeded? First, he made the decision not to be defeated by anything or anyone. Secondly, he decided to look for an opportunity, and as every successful person knows, just starting to look is the first opportunity itself. Thirdly, he found it. In crime, of all things.

Of course, crime is one of Britain's fastest-growing industries. But the biggest crime of all in the country is the talent that goes to waste through inaction – through simply not having the right attitude. Having combated the latter of these Chorlton took on the former.

The major reason that crime is rising so fast is not the number of burglaries, muggings etc. – the overwhelming increase has been in car crime. What better way to combat this than to distribute a product which makes you money in the process? Rule 1 in any basic business guide: sell a product that saves or makes other people money. Sounds simple? But the product, although good, is just the physical manifestation of one man's attitude.

The problem with Chorlton is that he can't keep his own success to himself. He wants to share it. He looks out for other people who are like he was, to join his organisation. He looks for people with a common cause – rule number 2 of the basic guide: who can help him.

This is what propelled him into network marketing. But he didn't go into the business to get rich. He went into it to change people's lives. Success breeds success. Chorlton believes that's what made Britain great and will do so again.

In fact, Chorlton is a great patriot and is very proud of the fact that the Nightstick, the anti-theft device, is manufactured in South Wales where he grew up. 'I was amazed that we could produce the product cheaper here than in Korea. It just goes to show that we can, and still do produce things of quality in this country. We sent the models and the basic concept to Korea and they were stumped with it. England is still the country that is coming up with the ideas but we just don't say it anymore. More people in industry must realise that we can do it here. There appears to be a massive lack of people like me.'

When this man speaks, it's well-nigh impossible to feel the doom and gloom that invades so many people's lives. Here is a man who turned the recession to his advantage by taking hold of the available talent and has created a multi-million retail empire in less than a year. Nightstick, the company, turned over £11 million in its first nine months.

'I'm really a retailer of products – I'm not in network marketing. Instead of having a very expensive retail chain I've used the people who are readily available in a quantity that I've never enjoyed before. I think it's a great system and in the next ten years, that will be proven beyond any doubt. Now it's my time.'

And it's not all about selling: 'I've seen the production of leaders – I look for that leadership quality in people. The reason this has been so successful is because I've locked into about 35 people and I've worked with them continually. We have a hard core of about a hundred and they would go through anything with me.' Even Jesus only had twelve disciples, but Chorlton insists on one hundred. Like J.C.'s men, they too come from a variety of backgrounds: lawyers, accountants – even people who have turned up holding Giro cheques. But there are certain qualities that bind them together: 'I look for people who have the time; they also have to be faithful and they have to be honest.' And once he has them, he is faithful in return. 'I'm not an egotist – I don't think that I know best. If it sounds good and it looks good, then I'll try it.'

He says that they don't just get loyalty in return: 'When cheques start coming through their letterbox for eight thousand pounds every month, then you know they've seen your point of view.'

But it wasn't all instant success – the company was believed to be doomed to failure. Chorlton was handed nearly 90 per cent of Nightstick by the former directors, and he and David Jacobs (who owned the remaining cut) turned it around in 1991. Clearly, you don't get taught this sort of thing in universities. 'No, it's more from the university of life, I suppose, although I hate that phrase,' says Chorlton modestly.

## Michael Dell – The Man Behind The Grin

Sitting in his black leather and chrome office suite high above the Texan freeways, Michael Dell looks too young for the trappings of executive status. No grey, no flab, no worry lines. Grinning amiably, he just doesn't look right somehow.

Dell started out life already at a level that many people aspire to. Born into an upper middle-class Texan family, he did well at school and won a place in medical college. If he had not started Dell Computer Corporation he would have been a comfortably-off doctor, living in the suburbs of Austin, Texas, by now. He could easily have accepted his family's aspirations and been moderately successful. But Michael Dell got bitten by a bug which wouldn't allow him to take the easy route.

Dell was brought up in a thrifty, industrious, clean-living, Jewish background. One thing there wasn't much of was risk, so at 18, after a year at medical college, he committed the middle-American sin of dropping out. At the time, people said he was mad. Why turn down a good career and secure background to work for yourself? He knew why.

In the words of Marie Curie, the scientist, 'one never notices what has been done; one can only see what remains to be done'. Basically, Dell wanted to do it himself from scratch. This may have been partly rebelliousness, partly foolishness, but soon Dell was selling computer disk drives to his old college chums. He would drive round their halls and take orders. As the business got bigger, he started to think about employing people and hit upon the idea which has made him one of America's most successful entrepreneurs: he cut out the middleman. Instead of recruiting dealers to sell his disk drives and computers, he decided to sell them direct to the customer and pass the dealer's margin on to them.

Over time he built the business up, being careful to recruit only the people he thought were absolutely necessary. After eight years in the business he was voted America's top Entrepreneur by *Inc. Magazine* and now is a Porsche-driving millionaire (dollars, but several times over). He often comes up against people who have had to wait for their success, considering it a right associated with seniority. They find him jumped up and aggressive. But what people

## The Unemployables

really dislike about him is that he's a bright chap, comes from a nice family and is happily married. He still follows his father's maxim, 'play nice, but win'. So how has he been so successful?

There is no secret to his ability. He knows everything there is to know about his products and he sells them constantly. 'He never stops selling,' says one of his close aides. 'Even when you go to a party, he's there making contacts, taking people's names and looking for business. He follows up every chance and never seems to get tired of it.' His company reflects the style. People are always 'talking up' the business and walk into his office whenever they want.

Another personal asset is his quick-wittedness. 'He just seems to pick things up faster than those around him,' says another manager. They say they can go to him with extremely technical business problems and Dell goes straight to the heart of the matter immediately.

It has to be said that although Dell has these personal qualities, he is by no means an experienced manager. Sometimes this makes him less diplomatic than he otherwise should be. Dell considers it an advantage not to have had any corporate experience; 'You don't need any preconceived notions in this business. I had a clean-slate approach to it which was helpful; because I didn't know how it was done in other companies, I just concentrated on doing it myself,' he says. Despite his comments, it seems that a few years ago his general lack of management and people skills caught up with him. Managers were fired or quit, profits came down and there were delays in new product introduction. His existing managers said that he had become a little too bossy and wasn't listening.

Dell is a little more circumspect about his learning experiences. During the same period when the company had its problems, Dell took time out to do a management course. This seems to have alerted him to the benefits of learning from others, rather than doing it the hard way. He visited Japan to see, first-hand, some factory automation technology. He also went to business school. 'I took a course at Stanford University and came back with a wealth of knowledge. It gave me an understanding of the concepts so that I can make investment decisions properly. Now I know enough to be dangerous,' he said at the time.

Nowadays, the business is more delegated. He relies heavily on the people around him. 'They must have the basic technical skills but I also look for people who add to the skills that I have.' Dell feels that his strongest skills are 'an understanding of the market, its channels and the product requirements of customers', but prefers to emphasise that it is 'a flat, highly responsive organisation that matters'.

'That's not to say that things don't still go haywire. When Michael's got a problem, all hell breaks loose until he has sorted it out. He'll just go round dragging people out of their offices all over the building,' says a close aide. It seems that one Michael Dell in the company is enough. There aren't any other young whizz-kids like him at anywhere near the same level. It seems Dell prefers the counsel of older and wiser men. This is perhaps testimony to a belief that, while it worked for him, it may not work for everyone.

Although it would be easy for him to be arrogant and aloof, having achieved so much so young, all his staff from the managing director to the toilet cleaner say that he can be easily approached. Even if Dell is bored stiff with talking to people he never shows it, always seemingly interested and helpful. There is probably method in this from the media point of view, because the more approachable he is, the more the media like to profile him. His grinning round face is to be seen on computer and business journals the world over, to the continual irritation of his competitors, who struggle for publicity against his wunderkind image.

The other thing he does to irritate his competitors is a lot of comparative advertising. Dell points out, feature by feature, why his product is better than the opposition's. Recently he went too far against one, Compaq, and they issued a writ saying that his advertising was deceptive. Dell was unrepentant, saying that he was flattered that Compaq thought he was a threat (they are roughly twenty times bigger) and that they could expect more of the same.

When he's not reading technical manuals, Dell's favourite publications are the *Economist* and the *Financial Times*. He also likes to read trade journals and local newspapers. When he's not reading, or selling, he and his wife, Susan, do voluntary community work. Dell feels strongly about the business of giving back to the community what you take out. This means that he serves on the Chamber of Commerce board of directors and works very closely with a local children's hospital. He is also heavily involved with the University of Texas and local elementary schools. This is a standard he applies to his staff by encouraging them to participate with volunteer support for local charities.

The most impressive thing about Dell is not so much what he himself does for the local community, but what he also insists the company does on his behalf. Through the corporation, Dell supports a charity programme called the March of Dimes, the Texas Special Olympics and a host of other local benevolent funds. Not satisfied with that, Dell Corporation also makes donations to the local opera, choral society and museum. In what little free time he has left, Dell and his wife go out on mountain bikes, go to the movies and travel.

By now the reader begins to get a picture of Michael Dell as being a super-sickly, super-hero whom several people have tried to undo. The problem is that it's all genuine. He is aggressive and commercial, but also amiable and sympathetic. This could be put down to an old-fashioned Victorian patriarchy. There's no doubt he looks after his staff, and there's no doubt that when Dell boy or Dell Corporation sponsors something, everyone knows. There's also no doubt that charity donations are tax-deductible. But if the individual can benefit the world and himself at the same time, where's the harm? If Bob Geldof made himself a little more famous by raising money for Ethiopia, why should anyone begrudge personal success gained from helping others?

The problem for natural entrepreneurs like Dell is that once they have developed an idea in one area, they want to go and do it all again elsewhere. 'It has been a very difficult thing at times, because there are so many good opportunities out there, but we have only so many laser bombs we can use,' Dell says, likening the whole thing to a computer game. 'We have to concentrate on optimising this opportunity before we can diversify,' he says.

He says that despite having achieved so much he is still as aggressive ever. 'I still have tremendous motivation and drive to build the company and make it as successful as possible. In fact, success has only increased my appetite.' If Michael Dell feels that he has missed out on anything over the last few years, he is not letting on. 'The things I couldn't do were more than offset by the things that I could.' Of the friends he left behind at college, he says, 'It is difficult relating to some of them now because their problems seem smaller. But I still keep in touch with them, we still have our past in common.'

What motivates him? He says he is not in it for the money, but then on a salary of £160,000 with a six-figure bonus and a personal shareholding worth around £50m, he would. He also says he never regretted floating the company on the stock exchange, just seeing it as 'widening the advice and the number of people who are rooting for you'.

Dell doesn't think he could have had the same success setting up in Britain, believing there to be 'too many cultural barriers to upstart companies like us'. He doesn't have too many role models either. There are people he admires but they tend to be leaders of other computer companies.

Dell makes competing in the jungle of the American business

world look easy. Being a little bit sharper than most, has allowed him to stay ahead of people who might otherwise be predators. If he displays the same ability fighting their legal cases as he does marketing his computers, the grin will be there for many years to come.

*The Unemployables*

## Daniel Field – A Cut Above The Rest

At fourteen, Daniel Field was an unhappy teenager. He suffered from acne and dermatitis, and had constant dandruff. He was small, weedy and none of the girls would talk to him. He ended up very depressed. Now he is one of the most successful hairdressers in London, is happily married, sells a range of hair-care products and has devoted followers such as Linda McCartney.

'I just wasn't prepared to put up with it,' says Field, 'so I went out and got myself a book on skin problems and worked it out myself.' Field discovered part of the problem was that modern shampoos aggravated his condition and what he needed was a 'natural' product. So he joined forces with a chemist and began making his own brews in his parents' greenhouse. He started off by making a gallon for himself, out of crushed lupins and tulips. 'I had to work with products which were available domestically that wouldn't do any harm. It took me a while to work out what oils would be similar and sympathetic to those in the body.' A few more textbooks later he came up with a shampoo that cured his dermatitis.

As word spread about his discovery he was approached by health food shops and some hairdressers to buy his product. Field was serving an apprenticeship in Raymond's in Knightsbridge, but the closure of this company coincided with an increase in demand for his own products. Soon business was brisk and Field thought it would be a good idea to set up as a hairdresser himself. His first shop, the Organic and Mineral Hairdressing salon, was opened in 1981 in North London.

There was an immediate demand for both the salon and for the haircare products that were used there. Surprisingly, much of the demand came from people who were working in other salons rather than from their clients. Field had spent a lot of time working in salons himself and knew that some of the chemicals used were dangerous and damaged people's skin. He therefore marketed his own products as much to people working in salons, as to their customers.

'It's really important to do what you're really interested in and ignore what people say. They all called me "pooftah" and "pansy" at school, but hairdressing is what I like doing and I've made a success out of it.' Field says he's not a natural businessman: 'I just like people. I enjoy talking to them and enjoy hairdressing.' Although he set up the business and spotted the market niche, it was his brother Mitchell who made the operation really profitable. 'I used to sit there thinking we would need so much money for this, so much for that, etc., and Mitchell would come along and say "why don't you combine these two and do it much cheaper?"

The business clearly has helped Field develop commercially as well as personally. A staunch family man, Field has been married since he was 20 and has two children and a large house in North London. He says he enjoys his work so much that he doesn't like taking time off, and even when he's not talking about the business he's thinking about it.

Field thinks about every aspect of the business constantly, especially what his customers feel when they walk into the shop. He says one of the most important things about being in a service industry, is that customers must be put at their ease. 'Some hairdressers try to psychologically downgrade people when they come in. They deliberately make them feel uneasy and ugly so that when they have cut their hair it suddenly feels a lot better. We want people to feel cheerful the minute they walk in and leave feeling they've got a great a haircut and value for money.'

For many customers, the ethics of the business are of no interest: 'Of course not everyone cares about the fact we don't test out products on animals,' he says. 'The main reason people come in is to have their hair done beautifully. Some people care about animals and the impact on the environment, but I think the reason for the success is a combination. People want to have experienced staff working on their hair; if they use natural products which are kind to them and the environment then that's a bonus.'

How does he feel about being called the next Vidal Sassoon? 'Well, all he did was to create a revolutionary style which everyone else copied. What we've done is something similar in terms of a revolutionary approach. I would rather be known as a combination of Sassoon and Anita Roddick (of the Body Shop) because she's a businessperson I really admire.'

Maintaining the standard of service is something Field is fastidious about. He even employs an agency that sends people round to have their hair done secretly and provide reports on how they were treated. 'It was a bit embarrassing because recently they came round when I was working in one of the salons. They said that I didn't talk to the customer enough. I was too busy doing their hair. It's a useful thing to know.'

## The Unemployables

The other thing he does frequently is to make notes on other service-based companies. He pays particular attention to how other people treat customers. 'There's a restaurant in London called Wolfe's and it's fabulous. The staff make you want to buy extras because they are so nice. Not surprisingly, they get big tips. I always take leaves out of people's notebooks. I try to give my staff the good points I've seen elsewhere.'

It was his brother who came up with the next idea for expanding the business. It is intended to sell the franchise of the haircare products to qualified retailers in much the same way as some of the other high-street retail chains have developed. This is something that will probably make Field a rich man.

Part of this is management skill and partly common sense. When Field originally set the company up he made sure he got some good advice about the structure. He decided to set it up immediately as a 'plc', which meant that he could issue shares and sell them if he ever needed to raise money.

Although Field is a young man, he has no intention of creating a dynasty; he says he will keep his family out of the business as it grows. Eventually he wants to see more of the world, but likes hairdressing too much to leave it at present. 'Running a successful business is just like a successful marriage. You start out naive and you learn about each other, you have your ups and downs, but if you're loyal to it the rewards you can get are tremendous. The successful people are those out there who really get to grips with their business. You have to get both arms right round it.'

'It's just about working with people. If people like you and they like the product, they'll always come back.' One of the examples of this is one of Field's early customers, an old lady who first came to him when she was ill. He offered to cut her hair for £2 to help her out. Several years later the lady still has her hair done at his salon, and Field never raised the price because he liked her so much.

This is not just marketing. Field knows what it's like to be an underdog and believes that money in business in secondary. 'It's not the money, I just like being a barber.'

## Sir Ranulph Fiennes – 'The World's Greatest Living Explorer'

'That's the way the *Guinness Book of Records* describes me; sounds corny doesn't it?' he says, slightly embarrassed. 'You get quite a lot of flak because the current fashion is for inverted snobbery which has been in fashion for a long time. People usually say it's quaint. In funny ways it's a drawback. They can be tempted to want to put you down because they think you're some jumped-up twerp of a peer. The problem with having a knighthood is that everyone thinks you're loaded or highly aristocratic.' Not so much the former, more the latter. Whatever he says, Sir Ranulph cannot claim to be from a working-class background. His father commanded the Royal Scots Greys, as did his father before him.

Fiennes' exploits with Dr Michael Stroud in Antarctica are well documented in a number of books, but few of these get to the essence of the man. Why does he do it?

If it was because Fiennes had problems living up to his father's reputation, that must now be receding. He left school with too few A levels to go to Sandhurst, but nevertheless joined the army and became a Captain. This is the title he prefers to use instead of his knighthood – 'It tends to carry more weight.'

Why become an explorer? Couldn't he have become a mercenary? 'Yes, certainly, but there's not much you can do to stop yourself getting shot. There's a helluva lot I can do to avoid falling through the ice.' He says the only reason he went into exploring was simply that it was the only thing he could do: 'The only application of the army training was in expeditions. Simple as that. My wife and I had been used to living on the breadline, but this was changed by the Trans-Globe expedition. I wrote a couple of books and made some films – then we were OK.' So he started to set up expeditions where he and a team of friends would go off with sponsorship from various companies. Without sponsorship Fiennes would not be able to do anything, and over the years he has had to become adept at getting media coverage.

'Television is the key to sponsorship – companies aren't altruistic, they want their pound of flesh. They have to calculate how much exposure their name is going to get in front of the cameras.' This, he says, is the hardest part of the exploration – getting people to part with sponsorship money. 'You have to be very thick-skinned because you're always asking people for money.' There are three sides to every expedition for Fiennes: charity, science and patriotism. The Prince of Wales is the Chairman of the fund-raising side of his activities. In 1990, Fiennes made £1.25m for a range of different charities.

Once he has the sponsorship, then he must find the right team. Although Fiennes is swamped with letters from young hopefuls wishing to go on his expeditions, he rarely selects anyone from outside his normal team: 'You have to be able to trust people with your life and that tends to exclude quite a few people. You have to be a good judge of character.' He is quite specific about the sort of qualities required from people: 'They must be good natured, non-malevolent, patient and then a long way behind those qualities comes their actual ability. We can make them physically fit, but the most important thing is that they have the basic personality skills. It helps enormously if they have a good sense of humour.' According to Fiennes, the most difficult people to deal with are the cameramen who are sent on the expeditions with them: 'The arty ones are the worst, they are really not cut out for it and they can be very tiresome.' This is understandable bearing in mind the way he lives. Fiennes is an early starter (he is at work by 6 am at the latest) and he drives himself incessantly. There is little doubt that he has an obsessive side to his character – he has to: when it's thirty below zero and the larder's empty you can't phone for a pizza.

When he's not exploring, Fiennes retires to his house on Exmoor, which is very remote with no mod-cons such as direct mains electricity supply. Since he has been there, he has become involved in a campaign to save Exmoor from building development. Does Exmoor seem dull after battling with the elements? 'Certainly not. It's a big issue saving these remote areas from being developed.'

Although Fiennes is cast in the mould of all the great British explorers – Livingstone, Scott, etc. – the hero has heroes and heroines of his own. Mrs Thatcher was one because she was a 'fighter'. His father was another. Fiennes says his father was one of the most influential characters on his life: 'He wouldn't let big problems – like Rommel – get him down. He always looked at tiny details and valued the opinions of all his soldiers and that helped him have a lateral approach to problem solving.' There is no doubt that Fiennes would have preferred to follow in his forefather's footsteps: 'If I had got my A levels, I could have gone into the army and done what my father did and commanded the Royal Scots Greys. That is my only regret.'

Fiennes' ultimate ambition was one of the few great polar achievements which were left. Strangely, he is coy about what he still wants to achieve just in case someone else 'knocks off' one of the last remaining unconquered feats. 'Of course there are the gimmicks like getting to the pole on a camel.' The ambition Fiennes fulfilled was to get to the South Pole and back unsupported, without back-up teams parachuting supplies in. This meant walking nearly 2,000 miles living on only what they could carry. It nearly killed him and Dr Michael Stroud, but they did it.

Fiennes has a bee in his bonnet about patriotism: 'Patriotism here seems to be a dirty word. It seems to flourish around Europe, in France and Germany, etc. People should try to buy British where they can. They must be made to understand that when they buy foreign they are exporting jobs. I can't understand it. They're like lemmings. For instance, Rover makes highly competitive cars, but people think it's fashionable to buy foreign.' Fiennes say that the British are too good at 'putting themselves down and projecting their worst sides of yobboes and idleness. There's not anyone in this country who cannot help the country of his birth by buying British. Patriotism is a wonderful thing, not jingoism. If you're born British, you should fight for your country in every way. If people say it's bad and things need to be changed, then they should fight and change it, not just moan.' He says that, although there are no more wars to fight, the British should still fight to take world records: 'You'd be amazed at the number of people whose days are made when a Brit wins a race or when England win a football match.'

Fiennes says he won't be the last great British explorer: 'There's loads in the pipeline and that's good. At least people who become explorers won't end up becoming drug addicts.' Does it worry him that the world might be running out of places to explore? 'No. Well, I'm not an introspective person, but there will always be achievements for man to strive for, either in the wilderness or at home.'

## Richard Gabriel – Delivering The Goods

Richard Gabriel went through it all. Betrayals, frauds, two recessions, you name it, he has thrived on it.

As successful Chairman of Interlink, the courier and delivery company, he looks back on it all with a maturity well beyond his years. 'When you go through so much, it makes you a stronger person. It's amazing what you can survive when you need to. Now I always think the best of people until I'm proved wrong. Everyone has potential.' And that's all Gabriel had when he started his business career at the age of sixteen. 'That was as a result of changing schools. I ended up just not covering the right subjects to sit the exams.'

With one O level, choices were a little limited. He decided to be a car mechanic because he had (and still has) a passion for fast cars. His racing ambitions would have cost him £10 an hour and as he only earned £3.80 a week he decided to seek fame and fortune in City finance. 'People say to you at that age, "What do you want to be?", but you can't possibly know – it takes a long time to think things out. I didn't have the faintest idea. But I knew I didn't like school.'

As a junior credit controller he managed to earn £14 a week, but it was still not enough. 'It became clear to me that hard work on its own was not enough.' Although he was coming up with lots of money-making suggestions in his various jobs, he wasn't seeing any of it.

He eventually ended up as a motorbike courier. Finally, he had found a place where his hard work paid dividends. By 1977, he was earning £300 a week. 'I am a natural early riser – usually between 5.30 and 6 am – and many a time I had already done a long-haul job before some of the other lads had got in.'

Then the inevitable happened – he fell off. But even this dark cloud had a silver lining, because he started to do some office work and realised he was being paid only around a third of what he was making. This is where he learnt the lesson that 'If you believe in your own skills you can get others to do the really hard work and reap the benefit of your own ideas.' He felt, though, that he was too inexperienced to go out on his own, and decided to set up another business with someone from the same company.

After a lot of work the company flourished, but soon afterwards

Gabriel discovered that his partner was driving round in a new Daimler, and what he had suspected for a time had happened. His partner was defrauding the business. So he sold his shares to him and left the business to set up on his own.

Interlink Couriers was to be the new company, if only he could get the finance. An important success factor in his career came to the fore at this time. His parents, who were from nursing and building backgrounds, offered not only the finance but the labour for the new venture. 'There's no doubt in my mind that they gave me my "hands-on" approach. My parents were extremely practical people. They have been tremendously supportive.'

Within six months, most of the staff from his old company had joined him, and his Daimler-driving ex-partner eventually went out of business. Gabriel's mother, Rose, helped in every aspect of the new company, going to see banks, running the office, even setting up the radio-control system.

Because Gabriel could not afford the staff to set up his computer systems, he taught himself how to program and did it himself. But as the business grew, he found he was becoming increasingly stretched. His main problem was how to get overnight deliveries of parcels to customers on time without taking on expensive full-time staff. It was then that he hit on the idea of using housewives as agents. 'I had been thinking in circles, and hadn't really thought about the problem laterally. It was an obvious solution.' So on 2 December 1981 Interlink Express started operating with 18 franchisees, as the housewives were known. He could not have picked a worse time. The snow fell and wreaked havoc with the business, but they struggled through. Worse still was a passing-off writ that was issued by another company called Interlink, which eventually went the same way as his ex-partner.

At this time, Gabriel was travelling 800 miles a week for the courier side whilst still trying to run the new parcels business. It was clear that a new computer system was needed to take the administrative workload off him. He took the risk and invested in an expensive system – and had just got it installed in his office when the killer blow hit. One night the office burned down taking with it all the company records, the office and the new computer.

Gabriel was woken at 7 am the following day by his finance director, who added for good measure that he had forgotten to renew the firm's insurance on the office and the computer.

Standing outside what was left of his office, he was a broken man. With typical pragmatism, he thought, 'Well, I'm hungry, I may as well go and eat breakfast – it can't do any harm.' Gabriel says that whilst he sat there eating a large breakfast of bacon and eggs, it suddenly dawned that although his office was out of business, he wasn't, and that there could be a chance of running all the systems manually. Soon everyone was lending a hand: his office neighbours supplied an extension lead which gave him enough light to work by; another office took his calls for him; and the staff all came back dressed in jeans to help clear up the mess. 'That's when you really find out if people respect you or not. There is a tremendous spirit in the office and people still look back on the fire and are amazed at what we achieved.' As it turned out, the building was mostly insured by the landlord and that covered the computer as well. In total, he lost only £100,000.

Gabriel says that coming through all the various storms has somehow helped boost loyalty in the company. 'We really do work like a family in more ways than one. But you have to show people the right approach. It has to come from the top. You have to give them their freedom. Nobody is too frightened to ask any questions or make suggestions about improving things. In many companies they take suggestions as criticisms, but we just give our people the authority to make up their own minds and have their say.'

Finding people who fit in with that culture can be difficult. 'We are always looking to hire attitudes and train skills. I don't think references are any good. I know myself you can make them look as good as you want.'

Gabriel keeps his staff motivated by publishing regular league tables of their performance and awarding prizes to the most successful. Staff wages are also kept low with substantial opportunities for them to double their salaries through their commissions. 'Some of my top people can hit annualised rates of £60,000 a year. But as long as they're bringing the business in, I'm happy to pay them that.'

Surviving traumas has become a way of life for Gabriel. Nothing stops him. 'In life you are faced with a limited number of opportunities which will come your way. But only a few latch on to them. Some don't even recognise them or see them for what they are. Sometimes the problems themselves present opportunities.'

His advice to would-be success stories is: 'Don't worry if your friends think you're mental – all mine did. You have to believe that you can do it yourself and that's enough. There's a lot of people who are in stressful, worrying jobs, but they never take the time to think about how they could change them. They've got their nose so close to the grindstone, they can't see any further. The main qualities of successful people are tenacity, enthusiasm, commitment to quality, and ability to get the job done.' The result of his philosophy is something that he is particularly proud of: 'In 1990 every UK parcel courier made losses except one,' he grins.

As his role in the business changes to becoming more of a strategist he is pleased that he can now enjoy some of the fruits of his labour. Gabriel lives in a large seven-bedroom house, and drives a Bentley and an Aston Martin and flies his own aeroplane. This is not to say that he now lives quietly. As happy on wings as he ever was on wheels, if life gets a little less than exciting he creates his own entertainment by flying down Loch Ness at 800 feet.

## Tony Gordon – Simple 'Self-belief, That's All.'

So says Tony Gordon, one of the most successful life insurance salesmen ever. Already a member of the Million Dollar Round Table (this is the club for the top 4-5 per cent of people throughout the world who sell life insurance), he has even attained the Top of the Table, which is the highest group within the organisation.

But it all started from very humble roots. A school drop-out at 16, he initially started working in the toy department of a retail store in Leeds. Then he got a job with Marks & Spencer, whose training he praises. In 1969, fed up with his prospects, he answered an advertisement which said: 'Nine-to-five men are two-a-penny. We want the exception.' He applied and got the job and thus began his career in financial services. This took him to Manchester where he worked for another four years before deciding to go to Bristol and set up on his own.

Since then he has never looked back. 'It took me eight years in the business before I really started to achieve any level of success. I went along, like many people in the business, just earning an adequate wage. The problem was that I'd only paid lip service to the setting of goals. I didn't have objectives, I was just wishfully thinking.'

Gordon says the most important thing is to break down the objectives into separate daily goals: 'I made up my mind that I wanted to qualify for the Million Dollar Round Table, but I thought it was beyond my abilities. I just calculated what I would need to achieve on a daily basis to make it. This meant going over my average case size and working out how many new ones I would need. At the time, this was a sale a day – four days a week. I organised myself so that I was seeing people Monday to Thursday with Friday to set up my appointments for the next week. I set myself a goal that I wouldn't go home on a Friday until my appointment book was full for the following week.'

Gordon says there's nothing complex about what he does. 'It's all about believing in yourself, that's all. You must have the courage to believe you can achieve your goals. Even if you don't achieve them, it's better to get half-way. If you aim at the stars and get to the moon, at least you have travelled. If you don't aim you won't go anywhere at all. You have to have the self-discipline to follow these goals through. I think I'm more afraid of failure than I am of the client, that's probably what drives me on. I think also I got some of this from my father, who gave me a sense of industry by working from 8.30 in the morning to 7.30 every evening, six days a week.'

Gordon believes that whatever job people do, they should want to be a member of any organisation which shows them to be the best in the business. 'We can achieve anything we want, provided we believe we can do it. The horizons we work under are all self-imposed. People are often just frightened of bigger prospects. If you believe your skill is worth it, then your clients will too. I know some professionals who charge £100 an hour and some who charge £50 an hour, and there's no difference in their abilities – just their own perception of self-worth. It's this self-belief that generates success.'

Gordon also has theories about why the success culture is lacking in Britain. 'Things have not changed much here since the Normans. Everyone knows their place, and everyone feels comfortable with their own class. There have been no changes in society for a long time. In America, everything is so new and there are no predefined structures. People find their own levels rather than the ones which they are born to. There is almost a resentment here towards success. This is understandable, because people don't feel comfortable when they get out of their own class.' Admitting that you are the cause of your own failure is one of the prerequisites for achieving success, according to Gordon. 'You have to be able to get up in the morning, look in the mirror and honestly say 'it was my fault that I did not achieve'. Once you accept the blame for failure, then you also realise you are the one responsible for your own success.'

He has a total fascination with human potential: 'No matter how good you get, you have to keep motivated. I'm always trying to work out whether this is the best I can be. If you're motivated, the people around you will be, too. The important thing to remember is that success is always relative to yourself – not to anyone else. To make this work you have to keep statistics of your own performance – that way you can keep things in context and measure progress. The real difference between success and mediocrity is self-discipline. Even the youngest salesman will say he hates prospecting. Well, so do I, but I know I have to do it because that's the price of success. There is nothing odd or false about wanting success, it's simply about using a little more of your potential. If you can do that, then you have succeeded.'

Another secret is not doing some things: 'The thing that successful people don't do is worry about the petty things in their life. A lot of people have a set of worries like those little machines you use for storing pound coins. They get rid of the worry on the top and the next one pops up to take its place. You've got to get things into perspective. The harder you work, the less worries you will have time for.'

Some of his personal motivation he ascribes to being a middle child. This, he explains, is 'not having the favouritism of the oldest or the youngest. So you struggle for attention and want to achieve to get people to notice you. There's a lot of successful people who have got what I call "middle child syndrome".'

He says that it's all about what you're used to: 'If you look at some of the immigrants in this country you will see that they have been incredibly successful, because they are used to having life really tough. Just having the freedom that this country affords is motivation enough to make them use it to the full.' For him, some of the first and second generation immigrants can be a real inspiration; and on this subject he says the best book he has ever read is Frank Bettger's *How I Raised Myself from Failure to Success in Selling*.

Although he is very enthusiastic about achieving his potential, Gordon knows when to stop. In 1984 he ran the London Marathon, just because he wanted to do it. He hasn't done it since, but it is typical of his approach: 'I wanted to do it, but I didn't enjoy it, so I didn't do it again.'

'It is important to be able to switch off sometimes. I'm not one of those people who feels they have to be working all the time. And I'm not driven to succeed at all costs. There is a big difference between working hard and being a workaholic.'

Gordon says that once people have had a degree of success they can easily get onto the slippery slope. 'It's really important to keep your feet on the ground. That's what my wife does for me. Some men like it if their wives butter them up and massage their egos, but it just makes them big-headed. She said to me, the minute I came home with a gold Rolex watch or a Rolls-Royce she would leave. You can tell when successful people have overstretched themselves; not only do they believe their own PR but their wives do, too.'

Gordon's philosophy is that being a self-made man is a good thing. Worshipping your creator is not.

## John Harrison – The Wilderness Years

Mosquitoes like helicopters, 57 varieties of malaria and those nasty, nasty things that burrow under the skin and lay their eggs.... Yet John Harrison, Amazonian jungle explorer in the great tradition, loves it all: 'It's a peaceful wilderness, where you really can be on your own. It's like nowhere else on earth.' Of course, others just see a stinking, rotting mass of vegetation devoid of every modern convenience.

Ever since he was a boy, Harrison has loved the outdoors and took every opportunity he had to camp out. His young mind was filled with great Tarzan adventures with stiff-upper-lip Brits hacking through the undergrowth. The nearest degree to his great passion was in Latin American Studies, which gave him the opportunity to see South America. In 1979, he was hitching on the trans-Amazonian highway, which runs straight across the Amazon basin, when he decided that things might be easier if he got a dugout canoe and travelled by river. With an Australian companion, he set out equipped only with his sense of adventure: 'The first trip was a total disaster. It was in the middle of the rainy season, and everywhere was so wet we had to sleep in the boats. Our food was washed away and we ended up living on raw fish. It was fairly populated though, so we couldn't get into much trouble.' By fairly populated, Harrison means that they saw a house or some natives every two days. When he got back to civilisation he was a few pounds lighter and a lot wiser.

Bitten by this and a hundred other species of bug, he decided to go back, this time in the dry season, which was more of a success. Not content to explore easy rivers, he began to try progressively more and more difficult and remote spots. He loves the challenge that the jungle can provide: 'It's a terrific feeling to go somewhere that no white man has been.' Of course, there are other humans in the jungle – wild Indians – who range from friendly to ferocious.

The great motivation for Harrison is the challenge of being self-reliant, attaining the objectives he sets and pitting his wits against the jungle. He says he finds the atmosphere very peaceful and serene – the sort of thing that is impossible to find in a civilised environment. 'You can still go for six months and 1,000 miles and not see anyone at all, so coming back can be quite intimidating at

## The Unemployables

first. You get very shy of people, the noise and the traffic. Crossing the road can be quite frightening.'

Harrison says the trips have taught him things he never would have learnt had he stayed at home. 'It's made me more tolerant and more resourceful. You only find out what you're really capable of when you're truly challenged. There are no noble characteristics to survival because instinct takes over. If I travel with someone, I'm always losing my temper with them – and I always regret it later. It may bring out strengths, but it reveals weaknesses as well.'

The reason he is so resourceful is that he finances his expeditions on a shoestring. If he were sponsored for large amounts then he would never really be independent. But costs are not everything: 'There's not much to spend money on in the jungle.' Although Harrison has had much interest and support from the Royal Geographic Society (of which he is a Fellow), he doesn't have much time for people who explore on a big budget. 'Some go off with all sorts of gadgets which make it too easy – a radio for instance. This means they can get a helicopter to pick them up in 24 hours if they hit trouble.' Needless to say he does not carry a radio, but he does have a very big first-aid box. If he were to break a leg in the middle of nowhere, he would set it himself, rest up for a few days and have it rebroken and set when he could. He says being able to cope on his own gives him great satisfaction: 'You're dependent on no one and it gives you a wonderful sense of freedom.'

It is just as well he enjoys self-reliance, because on seventeen different occasions in the middle of nowhere he has contracted malaria. He always has plenty of quinine and knows exactly what to expect: 'You get a temperature of 105, then you start to shiver, then you start to sweat and then you go raving on about all the secrets you wished you could keep to yourself – that's the worst bit.' It doesn't matter that he takes anti-malarial drugs before he goes out – there are so many different strains and it is impossible to avoid being bitten.

Malaria kills two million people a year, and is one of the biggest killers in the Third World, but Harrison says there are other dangers: 'Alligators, piranha fish and wild Indians, for instance.' The biggest problem though is getting lost: 'It is so easy to wander off from your camp to go and get a turkey for supper and not be able to find home again.'

People think that explorers are reckless, but Harrison says he is quite the contrary: 'Sometimes there is a temptation when you're tired to take on river rapids because it's easier than walking, but you learn to be careful. A lot of preparation and planning goes into my expeditions and I don't want to see that wasted.'

Harrison's longest trip, in 1983, was 1,000 miles in an attempt to cross a range of Brazilian mountains and drop down into French Guyana. Things started to go wrong: 'We didn't see anyone for five months, we were getting malaria every two weeks and we were almost out of quinine.' The trip ended in failure and he was on the point of giving up when he stumbled across an airstrip. 'There are times when you wonder what the hell you're doing...'

Self-discipline is essential in these circumstances, and Harrison puts great store by the preparation of a daily plan, including targets to be reached, rest days, etc. 'It seems to take on a great deal of importance when you're miles from anywhere. Even when the going gets tough, you stick by your plan, it's all you've got.'

At the end of each trip, he returns to his Bristol home and his wife, Heather, who has started to accompany him. He has no qualms about taking his wife; it may make him a little more careful, but he is a believer in sharing his ambitions.

When not exploring, Harrison is writing and doing carpentry odd-jobs to save up for the next trip: 'The years in the jungle have made me quite good manually.' His book, *Up the Creek, an Amazon Adventure,* was published in 1986 and was described by the London *Evening Standard* as 'a record of courage and endurance'.

Despite all the media exposure about the plight of the rain forests, Harrison says the message still has not sunk in about the rate of destruction. 'Most of the programmes preach to the converted; a lot still has to be done at government level.' With this in mind, he made a film about the Amazon for Central TV and *National Geographic*.

Part of his motivation for the trips is that he has a passion for natural history and wild life: 'You have to. When you're looking at 101 different insects sucking blood out of your arm, it pays to know which is which.'

## Tony Hawser – The Successful Reject

Tony Hawser was born into a comfortable middle-class background and was a qualified barrister by the age of 25. If he had carried on, he would have had a comfortable living, nice house, nice car, etc., but he wouldn't have been happy. Now, as Chairman of Reject Shop, he has all of that and happiness too. His high-street shops belong to a nationwide chain and sell a range of value-for-money, modern, home furnishings. Despite the name, none of the stock is reject.

So why did Hawser leave the cloistered environs of the law to go out into the rough, tough, vulgar world of business? 'Safety is never a requirement when you're 25; besides security is not particularly great as a barrister. Equally, business is not full of crocodiles, it's full of people who are prepared to help and admit their mistakes. My friends used to say, "What do you do for an intellectual challenge?" But great businessmen really think about what their market is going to be in a few years. Writing a company plan is also a difficult business. You can't foresee things like the Gulf War or changing attitudes – there are bolts from the blue.'

Good businesses are run by intelligent people, and Hawser is certainly that. 'Just because you've got qualifications doesn't mean you're necessarily intelligent,' he says modestly with a string of letters after his name. 'The most important thing is how you apply it.' Hawser reckons that if you took most successful people and educated them in any particular discipline, they would excel at it. 'Usually they are fast on the uptake, quick to spot an opportunity and work hard to master it. Academic education does not guarantee success these days. It helps generally, but you don't have to have it. Common sense will do.'

Hawser spends a lot of time in America, usually a month a year, and he watches the way people apply common sense to their business. 'For instance, in the supermarkets, the service here is atrocious and the quality of the merchandise is poor. There's always a queue. If there isn't a queue then the management think there are too many check-outs operating. In America, if the store manager is there, he helps pack bags as well. The chief factor is that the British buyer is prepared to accept it. In the US, you can walk into a store with a whole load of shopping and someone will come up and offer to carry it for you. It's basic common sense. You can make so much money just by being courteous, considerate and helpful.'

Apart from his pet hates about British service, he says it really is impossible to compare the two countries, because so many factors have to be taken into account. Attitudes though, he says, are comparable and they are distinctly different here. That was part of his motivation for changing things. It is easier to do well here, because fewer people are applying common sense.

Hawser has been very logical about expansion, tending to open shops along one geographical axis like Oxford, Bristol and Reading. This means there are economies of scale in servicing them. 'London may appear glamorous and wealthy but I won't do a store unless the terms are right.'

Hawser thrives on the long-term challenges of both the business and the economic climate: 'I see my role as being Chief Thinker. I perform a monitoring role. I watch things very carefully. The Chief role is just making sure that we're on the right lines. A lot of entrepreneurs tend to be good at selling but really poor at administration and that's what brings them down. You have to be good at each side, a bit like Gordon and Anita Roddick of The Body Shop. The former is the administrator, the latter is the saleswoman.'

Part of this thinking role is to know exactly what is going on around him. 'You have to be interested in the environment, because it affects you.

'I find it puzzling that a lot of people who went down in recession couldn't see the writing on the wall. There are rules that govern the growth of companies: when they break those rules, then they are either a genius like Roddick or, more likely, they will eventually go bust.'

The Hawser mentality is that if you have a successful formula – use it. 'I have very strict criteria for what I will do. Each shop has to conform to exactly the same figures. If someone else says they can do better, then let them try. They can have the site. I'm in no hurry to grow, there are plenty of hares for every tortoise.' Consequently, Hawser runs a tight ship from a small, dingy office on the top of a warehouse in Fulham. 'We are low-cost retailer and our prices are competitive. We don't spend an enormous amount of time trying to look like Harrods. We're not terribly grand, and our staff aren't hugely well paid. We're not trying to impress except by being friendly and efficient. If you want a business to adopt those ideas you have to live them yourself. We don't want our employees coming to head office and seeing money wasted.'

Hawser says that the successful entrepreneur has to keep an eye on the economy and understand what the long-term effects are going to be. 'We won't see more consumer boomerism. All our adult life we have accepted that house prices will go up, but we may have to get used to falling house prices, because they don't represent such a good investment anymore.'

The other thing he holds by is knowledge of the customer. Reject Shoppers are between 18 and 35, married, or just about to be, with one or no children. They have just bought their first property. They have cars and they are style- and value-conscious. More important though, he says, is that they want a 'street cred' buy.

Probably most important for Hawser is that everyone, from the boss down, enjoys themselves. 'If you want to succeed at Reject Shop, as in any other aspect of life, you have to be enjoying what you do. We like our staff and look after them. If you put me on a desert island I'd be happy with any of them. If you want to be successful, you have to have a desire to be unconventional to stand out from the pack. Like the guy at school who buys the chewing gum in bulk and sells it on. It's always people who have moved away from the pack. Of course, other people move away from the pack and become criminals. You have to be opportunist and make the most of chances as and when they come up. You have to believe in yourself. Everybody is an individual and has their own unique set of skills. This means they could excel at one thing which uses all those talents. Only the individual can know when that opportunity arises because it has to satisfy so many of those unique skills. They also have to be in the right place at the right time, etc. If it doesn't work, analyse where the mistakes were made and try again.'

The message is, not to worry if you try and don't succeed. After all, his success has Reject stamped all over it....

## Howard Hodgson – A Passion For Life

Howard Hodgson has been close to death for a long time. He says that when he was small he suffered from acute asthma. He fought for every breath. He fought to live. 'Everything else,' he says, 'was easy after that.' He later recovered and went on to make a fortune in, of all things, the funeral business. Tragically, at the height of his success came personal tragedy. His second son, Charles, was drowned at the age of three in a swimming pool accident. The realisation of mortality seems to make him value and use his life to the full.

Twenty years ago he was penniless and living in a tiny bedsit in Birmingham. Now the author of *How to be Dead Rich (a decade for Maggie and me)* reclines in his comfortable Knightsbridge town house and says: 'Success is nothing to do with star signs, it's more likely to be genetic or connected with the circumstances of your upbringing.' By anyone's standards, he has been phenomenally successful. He achieved all this within 15 years, because he was a drop-out until well into his twenties.

His story is well documented. He initially started out working in a factory by day and selling life insurance by night. In 1975 he rescued his father's undertakers' company with a £14,000 loan. How did Hodgson turn around his father's firm? 'I sold my house and persuaded the bank to extend the firm's overdraft by £5,000.' The bank agreed, partly because he was resigning a £30,000-a-year life insurance job to do it. He then applied the same principles that had made him a successful insurance salesman. At his first meeting with the bank, the manager said he wanted to close the company down. Hodgson persuaded him not to. Under his stewardship, the company grew to take over several other funeral firms. At one stage he was responsible for burying one in ten of Britain's dead. He eventually floated the company on the stock exchange.

Recently, he retired from the funeral business, which he left with £6 million and a £350,000 pay-off. He now believes he has reached 'half-time' in his career. He put £200,000 on one side for new ventures and invested the rest: 'I just didn't want to wake up at 45 and find I'd lost it all.'

The decision to retire was prompted by a recurrent back problem

## The Unemployables

which he decided to have sorted out once and for all. Sitting in the hospital he made up his mind to do something else. Now he has formed a range of new businesses, one of them is Hodgson & Partners. This he describes as simply a business consultancy which aims to help smaller and medium-sized businesses to catch the first wave of the economic upturn. He says that companies are more likely to take advice from people who have been entrepreneurs themselves than from bankers. The company offers advice ranging from drawing up business plans, building management teams and acquiring finance.

Hodgson believes that everyone can amass huge fortunes if they want to and to prove this he has written his book. He attributes his own success to Margaret Thatcher and personal determination. 'The most important thing is the inner motivation to succeed. It's up to everyone to make what they can of their life.'

Why is he so successful? Most of it is his own doing. Some of it is lucky chance. One of Hodgson's traits is that he gets incredibly enthusiastic about projects, often working late into, and sometimes right through, the night. The other secret is from his upbringing. He was sent to school, high in the Swiss Alps, to cure his asthma. 'The school was run by a housemaster from Gordonstoun. There were lots of cold showers and fresh air. They didn't beat you up – they just forced you to run up mountainsides.' Although he plays down this experience, he was mixing with the boys of well-off families like the Burtons and the Cadburys. The discipline this gave him shines out. He is not intimidated by anything or anyone and still recognises the virtue of being well-connected.

The other contributory aspect is that he looks good. He looks the part of the successful businessman (although it is difficult to know what his longish hair would have looked like under a black topper). He has remained young in terms of appearance and style. Only under the closest scrutiny can anyone see the real story etched on his face.

He also has the gift of making people think he has opened a little window just to talk to them alone. People can't help liking him and he likes media exposure. Some of this no doubt came from his father who was 'a gushing personality, who was flamboyant and inspired great confidence'.

It seems that, because of his asthma, he knew that physical strength would never be enough alone. He therefore made up for that by sheer hard work. He often pulls his executives together on Sundays to give them a team talk. To them, there is no doubt that he has inspirational qualities to impart. There is little doubt also that a turning point has been reached in his life with business taking less of a role. Hodgson's passion for life can inspire people in many ways, not just in business and it seems he is now recognising this. He has presented one TV programme so far, and has a strong desire to do more. He seems to constantly look for other outlets to inspire, create and change the way of life of many individuals.

Although he has yet to fully apply all of his talents as a communicator (at which he excels), he is going about it in the same methodical way he did in funeral directing. It seems clear that success in this area can only be a matter of time. As surely as Hodgson the hippy turned into Hodgson the high achiever, his next identity is within his grasp.

The way he attains his goals is straightforward: 'There are four things for succeeding in business: you have to like it; you have to be good at it; it has to be able to make money and it has to be sustainable in the long term; and you must be able get people you like and respect and trust to run it.' He attributes his personal success to 'a little chap sitting on his shoulder who drives him on and tells him to do things'. He may like to be liked, but he doesn't actually care what people think. He believes too much in himself for that. And that is another key element: 'You can keep running into cul-de-sac after cul-de-sac, but you can still succeed just by having an inner belief. It's the sort of thing immigrants had when they first arrived at Ellis in New York.'

This is applied to his basic philosophy: 'If you have your name on something you must want it to be the best. And if you work harder at it than anyone else, it will be. The ball really is in your court. Look at the number of Ugandan Asians that have come here and done really well. People just make too many excuses for not achieving. You have to say "OK, let's go". If you start off with a view to just making money, you'll probably make some, but you won't make a lot – you have to have a passion to succeed.'

It is almost pointless to list his other passions because there is very little he doesn't feel passionate about. England, his wife and children, Ian Botham, sailing, watching Aston Villa, and of course the Beatles (he even wrote a book about John Lennon and Paul McCartney). His fascination with the Beatles seems to have been driven by another root desire to be noticed and to be famous to pop-star proportions. He may not be as well known as Paul McCartney, but he certainly has the lifestyle. He lives in Knightsbridge, has homes in Dorset and the south of France and has a yacht and a speedboat. The astonishing thing about Hodgson is that although he has been very successful already, it really seems that there is so much left that he will achieve.

*The Unemployables*

The essence of the man is an indomitable will, with a huge appetite for life. This is the sort of stuff that Douglas Bader was made of. And his message is: if you want to succeed, you have to be passionate about it.

## Grace Igwe – Mother, Teacher, Entrepreneur

Grace Igwe is coy about her age, because she thinks that people hold to much store by age: 'It's not important how old you are, it's what you do with the time you've got left that counts.' This is typical of a comment that comes from someone who started their first business at the age of 61.

Grace Igwe was born of wealthy parents in Nigeria. She grew up with the trappings of colonial splendour and was sent to England to be educated. After completing her education, she went on to become the first ever black debutante on the London social circuit. This led to a career in modelling. Grace Igwe was modelling clothes for Selfridges a long time before the age of super models.

She talks about this period of her life as if it was insignificant, but to someone who has achieved so much else in her life, it is. She returned home to become personal assistant to the President of Nigeria just before the Biafran war broke out. This was the most unhappy period of her life. 'I had to watch my country being torn apart by itself. It was tragic. When the war was over there were several members of my family that I had to bury – that was very hard.'

Grace played a major role in helping rebuild Nigeria after the war. This was not just tea and sympathy; she personally drove a 34-ton truck around and can recount stories of having burying people with her bare hands. By this time she was married, and was bringing up three children. Her husband was a religious minister who was preparing to go on a mission to England. And so Grace become the first ever black missionary to come to England.

She settled in Cheshire and found the locals less than welcoming. 'Before I moved in I had people – quite senior people – coming to me and telling me not to do my cooking outside because the residents wouldn't stand for it. But it was a reaction I was prepared for.' Grace says that although she experienced real racism from English people, she bore them no ill-will. 'They didn't know any better. Most of them actually thought that I would be cooking my food outside on a camp fire. It was quite amusing really.'

Shortly after this, she was asked by UNESCO to form a village of children from all over the world. The Global Village was created in

1964 and was a tremendous success with six children being sent from every nation on earth.

Her next great achievement was in Geneva, where she raised £25m for charity with a variety of activities. At the end of the seventies, she returned to England to take up a role in teaching. First she was at Haringey in London, then at Sheffield in Yorkshire, where she rose to become headmistress.

After seven years of teaching, she decided at the age of 61 to go into business and within three years had built a company that was turning over half a million pounds a year. She called this Grace International, and now the business is based in three continents and supplies executive gifts and a range of interior decorations and household furnishings. She does not think that it's unusual for someone who has a had a background in education and religion to go into business. 'Basically the same skills are required in each. You have to be able to organise people and get things done. Perhaps the most important skill is that of being able to persuade people of your point of view.'

Grace says that although she has been an achiever all her life, the business has been one of the least demanding things she has done. 'The Biafran war was the hardest thing for me because it was a personal as well as a national tragedy. Once you've been through something like that, you can go through anything.'

At the age of sixty-something many people would be thinking about winding down into their retirement, but not Grace Igwe. She has been offered a cabinet advisory post and is gearing up with further plans for expanding her business. 'Age is not the important thing about your life. It's your attitude that counts. If you think like a sixty-year-old then you are sixty. Me, I'm still a teenager. I like to be surrounded by children, they keep me young.'

Grace believes that one of the keys to success is knowing when you're well off. 'Once you've been through a war, you soon get to feel quite privileged if you've got your basic health and a roof over your head. There are too many people that take what they've got for granted. They should try travelling around a bit to see how other people live.'

Grace is of the opinion that most people's problems or unhappiness are caused by the fact that they think about themselves too much. 'When you start living for other people, you stop thinking about yourself and all the energy then goes outwards to others. That's one of the most precious gifts you can have.'

## Colin Jackson – 'I'm Gonna Be The Best And That's That'

The best in the world is all Colin Jackson wants to be. 'I just made up my mind that's what I wanted. It never really occurred to me as a kid, because I was just running for fun. But I never really wanted to do anything else.'

To be the best takes long-term as well as short-term tenacity. Every day, Jackson subjects himself to a gruelling exercise regime which takes three hours. He usually does this in the evening, because doing it in the morning would create too high a risk of injury as it takes a while to warm up properly. It doesn't leave a lot of time for anything else. 'After training I just go home and die. It's just about all I can do to have a shower and watch TV. Maybe by about midnight I'll have recovered; then I do some paperwork until one or two in the morning.' The training exerts such a strain that he spends a lot of time sleeping: 'There just aren't enough hours in the day to sleep.'

The discipline he needs is enormous. He has to be careful about what he eats because he has to maintain a constant racing weight. His trainer, Malcolm Arnold, sets him an annual goal which is broken down into monthly and weekly objectives. 'He doesn't have to push me too much because he knows that I'll work for it.'

Although the regime never varies and there can be no holidays, he never lets up: 'I never get sick of it, because I really enjoy it. I know there are no shortcuts. I really don't need any other motivation – I know what I want and I know what I have to do.'

Jackson never really started out with the intention of being the best in the world: 'You just win a race one day and find that you're in that league. But when you do, people's expectations change and you suddenly gain new responsibilities.' He has had to put up with playing second fiddle to some of the more established stars like Linford Christie, Daly Thompson and Tessa Sanderson, but his star quality is growing. The bogeyman which might stop him is injury. 'So far I've been lucky. I haven't had any muscular injuries since 1988, but that doesn't mean no injuries at all. They are a constant hazard.'

He believes there's not much psychology involved in training or

## The Unemployables

racing. 'All that stuff's tripe. You just have to work hard to be fitter than anyone else. There's no doubt that drugs are an easy option, and it's a simple trap to fall into when you're trying to squeeze that last bit of performance out. I can understand why people do it. But they're cheats.' He says that people take drugs because it is so very difficult to be a world champion: 'Everyone wants success, but they don't realise what's involved. They don't know what it takes to be a winner. It's the toughest thing in the world. That's where my family and friends come in. They're very supportive and they come and cheer me on.'

Jackson says his life is too hectic to have a girlfriend because 'It wouldn't be fair. But when I do decide to settle down, I'd like to go to Canada and raise my family there. Things are a bit too static here.' He loves Canada and has just finished buying an apartment there. 'It's a new country. There's lots of space and plenty of opportunity. But I won't go until it's time for me to retire when I'm 33 or 34.' Would he marry another athlete? 'No. I'd like to marry a civilian. Whitney Houston will do!'

Jackson lives in Cardiff where he was brought up, but he still considers his roots to be Jamaican. His great hero is the Jamaican sprinter Don Quarry. 'There's a great bond between all Jamaicans – we're all just supertalented! No, seriously we have to fight a lot harder for our successes, even if you're born here. For people that came over and did well, that's even more of an achievement. They came over to the cold, the wind and the rain and still managed to carve out a life for themselves. That gave them the killer instinct to achieve. Both my parents have got that and so has my sister. My father is a supervisor in a local firm and my mother is a nursing sister. My sister and I get our good looks and modesty from them!'

Jackson's sister had just finished a contract with Channel Four's 'Brookside' and has a successful career in the theatre, 'despite there being few roles for black actors. She just stuck at it ever since she was a kid.' He says he wouldn't trade jobs with his sister, because sport is one of the most enjoyable careers around: 'I always encourage young people to go into it because they'll make so many friends. You also get a buzz out of making your parents proud of you.'

Does the sportsman do any other sports? 'I like playing squash and, being a Welshman, I like watching rugby, but I don't have the energy to do anything else.'

Jackson's approach can be summarised by his enthusiasm and commitment: 'All you need to do is work hard. You can't do anything unless you commit your heart and head to it. Then you'll make it.

You have to be in it simply for the achievement. Even if I didn't make Olympic Champion I would consider everything else in my life to be a bonus. You have to say to yourself: I'm gonna be the best and that's that.'

## Sir John Harvey-Jones – Product of Empire

'Everything I have learnt teaches me that it is only when you work with, rather than against, people that achievement and lasting success is possible.'

To describe Sir John Harvey-Jones as successful is a bit like saying Mother Theresa is helpful. If this man was a bridge, he would have been built by Isambard Kingdom Brunel – solid, sensibly constructed, practical and down-to-earth. Achievement is a 'must have' factor for him. He admits it, saying that he always felt the need to impress his unaffectionate father. In one way or another, he has been trying to get attention from people ever since.

It is difficult to pick which part of Sir John's life to highlight – it has all been pretty eventful. Naval college, submarines in the war, climbing the ladder at ICI, knighthood, media darling and, if rumours are to be believed, politician.

He was born in Hackney in 1924, but brought up in India and, at the age of six, sent to prep school in England. Strangely enough, here the industry stalwart sobbed and was beaten regularly by masters, often 50 strokes at a time. After this savage regime, the Navy seemed like a cakewalk and he went straight to Dartmouth Naval College at the age of 13.

There is no doubt that the Navy taught Sir John many of the management techniques that he was later to apply at ICI. During the war he served as a submariner and this was to leave its special marks too. He still has a habit of speaking bluntly, augmenting every other word with 'bloody' this and 'bloody' that. His long hair and unkempt appearance he attributes to two aspects of the Navy: 'I was a submariner, which created a degree of insensitivity to some of the finer points of life and smell,' he says. Sir John also has a love-hate relationship with authority. In his early career in the Navy he hated it, and later, when he left, he rebelled by growing his hair long and wearing flowery ties. These have since become his hallmark.

The war was to teach him much about leadership. He cites one illuminating example: his submarine had come to a halt in shark-infested waters with a blockage in a side vent. It had to be cleared so he asked for volunteers; not surprisingly, none of his crew wanted to be shark-snack. So he went over the side himself. His crew joked about it afterwards but this precedent was to be repeated at many later stages in Sir John's career.

It was the war, he says, which also coloured his attitude towards the Japanese. For many years he feared and misunderstood them, and he says that it wasn't until he travelled there that he got over it.

He met his wife, Betty, whilst in the Navy. She was a radio operator. His comments betray the loneliness and craving for female company that built up from months at sea. 'I gazed across the room, the first thing I became aware of was the most glorious pair of legs, which belonged to the most exquisite creature I had ever set eyes upon.'

After the war he joined Naval Intelligence, his Russian speaking skills an asset for fighting the Cold War. He still cannot talk about this period. Shortly after this, his first child was born. Gaby was crippled with polio and osteo-arthritis. The Navy refused him compassionate leave to look after her, so he resigned his commission. She later had a grand-daughter Abigail, and Sir John looks after her as well.

In civilian life he joined ICI, as many of his friends had done, and his skills allowed him to rise up the ladder quickly. From 1982 to 1987 he was chairman of the company, and during this time he made the company highly profitable.

As far as money is concerned, he did not have an excess of it until the last decade. 'People find it difficult to believe that my wife and I did not own a car until we were thirty, and that it was only after I left the Navy that I had enough money to put a downpayment on a house.' He also says that he doesn't enjoy the success and the power. 'As power grows, so does the chorus of flattery. Some is obvious and sickening, but much is invidious. In common with many people I am vain, and would like to like myself,' he says.

Sir John's style is analytical – he wants to know what this does, what that does, what effect does this man have, etc. – and it was this that made him a household name through the national TV programme 'Troubleshooter'. This was a series where he visited a number of companies to tell them what they were doing wrong. The show got some of the highest ratings ever on the BBC.

There's no doubt that his success with the media has made him enemies, being called 'the biggest bullshitter in the business' and 'the Great I Am' by critics. This perhaps reflects a belief amongst senior industrialists that they should stay away from the limelight. However, Sir John's style is visible leadership from the front. He feels this is an essential part of good management, not being afraid to be seen.

What secrets can he impart to those further down the greasy pole?

## The Unemployables

'Find interest in the most mundane of things,' he says. His belief is that detail can be fascinating. When asked by someone why steel girders, for instance, were interesting, he rounded on them, saying, 'What's the matter with making steel girders? You think it is dead dull. Making steel girders is extremely interesting.'

He believes that unless people progress all the time they are moving backwards: 'There is a certain sadness in this environment as few, if any, marks are awarded for effort.' He thinks people are self-motivated and that 'they do their best work when they come to believe through their own processes, that what they are doing is worthwhile'. He believes people have an immense capability when expected to perform in extraordinary ways. This is a philosophy he has applied to himself: 'I personally have always liked the 100 per cent aspect of life; I have always enjoyed life at the extremes,' he says.

In the meantime, Sir John still leads his heady media life. He lives in a Grade I listed manor house in Ross-on-Wye, Herefordshire, where not surprisingly the furniture is oak and the bed is very expensive.

Without doubt, Sir John is a product of the Empire. Strong, practical and resourceful but with underdeveloped emotional machinery. He still says he finds it difficult to open up to people – 'The fear of being thought a sissy goes very deep.' He is still very much a man's man, and finds it difficult to understand why women don't like being called 'girls'. It is, however, easy to forgive him these prejudices, because very likely he will try to get rid of them if he thinks they offend. 'I have spent my life trying to become the sort of person I would like to be.' This means, according to a recent interview, a sort of boy's own paper character. The typical British gentleman who is strong, courageous, and compassionate. Successful enough to be satisfied, ambitious enough to be motivated.

## Kevin Harrington – Reformed Troublemaker

Kevin Harrington, the schoolboy, was the sort of Just William character that would pull little girl's pig tails and put toads in teacher's bag: 'I found school a complete waste of time. I got the cane every week for two years.' It has to be said this was quite a deliberate policy on his behalf. 'The way the system worked was that if you got detention once, you stayed behind. If you got it again, you got the cane and that was the end of it. So if I got detention once, I made sure I got it twice.'

Needless to say, he graduated from the school of hard knocks with some clear attitudes on the shortcomings of education. 'You have to cultivate troublemakers because they are true individuals. At least they've got the courage to step out of line. But the system doesn't work like that. Schools suppress talent and never really seek to find out what kids are good at.'

Kevin Harrington, Managing Director of the publishing house Harrington Kilbride, is the child writ large. Not surprisingly, he sent his own kids to private school: 'I bring my kids up totally different. They have much more freedom.' He believes it is essential always to tell children they can have anything. 'If people say "look at that flash car. It's OK for them, they've got money", a kid gets the impression that they can never get those things. But if you say "look at that flash car – work hard and one day you'll have one of those" – now that's a different matter.' Well, he now has worked hard and has a few flash cars. And when their windows get smashed (as they occasionally do) he tries to understand that it's usually bored kids who are only doing pretty much what he used to.

It was, after all, only 15 years ago that he launched himself into the magazine publishing business. He'd worked for a few small publications before, but then went into a partnership organising events for sporting activities with two older partners who were in their fifties, and the business grew out of that. 'The problem is at the age of twenty-one it's impossible to get people to take you seriously. But the trick is to start early, then you don't have any inhibitions. There are so many people in this country who can, but don't, for whatever reason.'

Harrington says that one of the most important things he's learnt is not to try to do everything yourself: 'People say they can never find anyone who can do the job as well as they can, and that's rubbish. You have to delegate the task and give people the space to do it their own way. A lot of people are talented and I try to let them do it their own way. You have to make people proud of themselves.' But it's not always that easy: 'It's very important for my staff to display initiative' – he likes people who turn up and ask for a job. Sometimes when sales people turn up and ask, he will deliberately say no to find out whether they are any good at selling. 'Anyone who takes no for an answer is not for us. They have got to have a bit of fight in them and try to sell themselves. If they say "well OK" and leave, we know they're not right.'

Harrington had the job of sales manager open for four years before someone came in and took it. 'You can only encourage people so much. At some point they have to show they want it.' That man now earns £150,000 a year – 'and he's bloody worth it,' says his boss.

'We have people working here most evenings until midnight. They enjoy it. Qualifications are not important, but I do have to feel comfortable with them. I want to make sure that even if I don't like them personally, they have to be able to fit in with their working group. If they can't do that, then it doesn't really matter how good they are.'

The importance of staff enjoying themselves cannot be overstated for Harrington. 'One thing we never do is yell at our staff. We just don't do it. We're all on first name terms. If people make mistakes, that's fine as long as they learn. If they have a problem they can come to me and tell me. If they don't do that, then they will be in trouble.'

The style certainly appears to be democratic. Harrington is soft-spoken, relaxed, but quite focused. He is the sort of chap that, if he did have to shoot off your kneecaps he would be very sorry and break the news to you gently.

Apart from spotting good people Harrington is also good at spotting trends. He watched the Berlin Wall come down and thought there would be opportunities to be had in Eastern Europe. But instead of just thinking about it, he did it. He launched four European magazine titles in quick succession, the advertising revenue for which was derived entirely from outside the UK. No middlemen, no third-party distributors, no one to dilute the profit. 'Everyone will say you can't do your own distribution, you have to go to a third party. That's just the way the big boys have got the market set up. You don't have to do it the same way as them. If you see a good way of doing it, then do it. Don't be put off by what people say. There are so many people who will give you advice. But I always ask "Who are they?", "What have they done?" I only take notice of those people that talk from a standpoint of experience. There's loads of people that know it all on paper – but not many that could do it themselves.'

One of the clever examples of this individual approach is illustrated by Harrington's Singapore printing operation: 'It saves about a third on costs.' Yet this is something that other magazine printers in Britain would never consider.

Harrington's big picture of the world is extraordinary, considering he has a fairly humble background. 'Well, I went to Ireland a couple of times when I was a kid, but my parents still live in a semi and find it quite difficult to relate to all this.'

The next big target for Harrington is South Africa. As the country becomes rehabilitated politically, many believe there will be a major economic boom.

Harrington's business grows by 30-40 per cent per annum, year in year out. 'The way we do it, is just to grow at a modest rate – once we've done our 30 per cent or so, then we start thinking about next year. We don't try to cram all the growth into one year. That's where I get my kicks – planning to get the next 30 per cent.'

For Harrington, the money is simply a by-product of success: 'All my time is spent at work. I love it. I can do what I want. I've got freedom and control. If I don't like something, then I stop it. I could never just be a manager. I want to make the thing grow. And if I don't have the skills I can hire them in.'

He does allow himself some indulgences, such as about 700 bottles of fine wine and regular nights out at the theatre. He also has a comfortable Aston Martin sports car. After being caned for two years on the trot (so to speak), it's probably a medical requirement.

## Lennox Lewis – The Importance of Not Being Afraid

In some respects, there is little difference between Keith Chorlton and Lennox Lewis. They are both from poor backgrounds, they are both fighters and they have both been successful. They have both known what it is like to have nothing – therefore they are not afraid of losing. This means that whatever happens, they end up as winners.

Lewis was born in West Ham in the East End of London in 1965. When he was seven, his mother went to Canada while Lewis remained with his brother Dennis at home in London. At the age of twelve he moved to Ontario, Canada, where he took up boxing on the suggestion of his school principal.

'I used to get into trouble at school. Kids used to bug me about my Cockney accent,' he says in an interview with *Boxing News*. 'During my first sparring session this kid hit me on the nose and my eyes watered. I thought "This isn't for me", but one week later we renewed our rivalry and decided to settle it in the gym the proper way.' The tears were worth it. Lewis won his first major prize in Canada at the Ontario championships. It was then that he began to take the sport seriously. At seventeen, he represented Canada for the first time and won a gold medal at the World Junior Championships in the Dominican Republic in 1983.

Lewis says he learned a lot from watching others like Ali. 'He can inspire me as a fellow boxer as well as millions of potential fans.' And before competing in the Olympic Games the following year, Lewis trained with Mike Tyson – a smaller Tyson at the time. From then the boxing career almost seemed a formality.

After winning the Super heavyweight gold medal in 1988 for Canada, Lewis and his mother returned to Britain and signed on with manager Frank Maloney in 1989. It was just a chance meeting that led to him taking up with Frank Maloney, a man who had been in the fight game since he was eight years old. 'I met Lewis by chance. I was trying to break into big-time boxing. Lennox was in Las Vegas talking to the promoters and I thought here's my chance,' Maloney says. There is a lot about Maloney that would warrant a separate chapter in this book and it has to be said that Lewis has obtained some of his positive attitude from his manager.

Although his move to England brought Lewis a lot of criticism, the fighter is no fool – it sped up his career towards a title fight so he avoided spending years boxing on the American circuit. Some say that he should have avoided a major fight and waited for a world title shot, but Lewis protests that it would have meant waiting another three years. 'In this case, I can feel how much the British fans want me to succeed. They desperately want a heavyweight champion.' It's been over 25 years since Britain has had a champion at that weight, so that isn't surprising.

'Coming back to England and taking what is rightfully mine (the British Commonwealth and European titles) made a lot of other boxers who had grown up in England jealous. They said a lot of things about me – "I'm not English" and "I don't live in England". It's just jealousy. But as far as the fans are concerned, they look on me as one of their own.'

This is a man who is in a hurry for success. 'Lewis is self-motivated. He sets his targets and aims for them. He is a real leader – he motivates the rest of us,' says manager Maloney.

It has to be said that Lewis's performances so far have been dramatic. His first professional fight was typical. It was against the Midlands area champion, Al Malcolm, at the Albert Hall. Lewis dispatched him in two rounds. Knocked out. Cold.

'When it comes to the fighter, I think Lewis is a tremendous example to the youth of this nation – he is dedicated and determined. He has no programme for failure at all – I don't think it's even mentioned in his head,' Maloney says. 'No one in the camp is allowed to mention the word failure or losing. Around him everyone is really positive.'

Part of Lewis's success formula is the attention to detail. For instance, Lewis arrived in London only two weeks before the fight with Razor Ruddock and trained on American time. This was to ensure that his body clock was not changed during the run-up to the big fight. He's already done training at Caesar's Brookdale-On-The-Lake Resort, a honeymoon hideaway in the Pennsylvania foothills. But he doesn't go there for the heart-shaped beds and sunken bath-tubs. His trainer, José Correra, who's taken Lewis under his wing, had him sparring with the best: former WBA title holders Tony Tubbs and Mike Weaver. And part of the training includes mentally psyching himself for the fights: 'Sure, he'll try to take my head off, but he can't do that to everybody. His power doesn't really concern me because he's been boxing shorter guys – guys who box differently from me,' is typical of the routine.

## The Unemployables

'Who else is there for me to fight? Every young prospect goes through a similar dilemma. Are his opponents too easy? Is he being rushed? With me there are a lot of unanswered questions, all of which will be sorted out in the next few fights,' Lewis has been quoted as saying.

Boxing is seldom ambiguous in its confirmation of success and failure. Draws are rare. It tends to attract people who equally want to win and who are not afraid to lose. Some people are too afraid of the latter to have a go at the former. Consequently, they commit the worst sin of all.

## Sophie Mirman – Typist Turned Tycoon

Sophie Mirman started out with no qualifications, at the age of seventeen, in the typing pool of Marks & Spencer. She ended up leading the high-street chain Sock Shop before it went bankrupt. Now, in her thirties, she is running a small children's store on the King's Road in London.

Perhaps as good as her own story, is that of her mother and father. They were a French couple whose parents did not approve of them getting married. They therefore decided to elope to London, where Sophie was born. Neither could speak a word of English, yet they set themselves up in the hat business, eventually making them by appointment to the Royal Family. Mirman comments: 'I was not artistic in the slightest, so I couldn't really follow in their footsteps, but I was always encouraged to work for my pocket money. This is where I draw my instincts from. My mother always worked and so did I. So I went into the typing pool at M & S in 1975 and I hated it.'

This was in fact one of the first lucky breaks, because it turned out that typists were rotated on assignment throughout the company and Mirman was sent to work in the executives' offices. On the first day, Lord Sieff, the Chairman, asked her what her ambitions were and she replied 'To be the first woman on the board at M & S'. This rather pleased Sieff, who took her under his wing and made sure that she received full training in the various departments of the company. The reason she appealed so much is still clear to see. She is bright, positive and full of energy – qualities anyone is capable of displaying.

She developed from here into store management. After six years, she'd had a good grounding in retail trading, and wanted to apply her skills to a fresh challenge. This came along in the shape of Roy Bishko, who set up Tie Rack. In 1981 she joined him as General Manager on a salary of £12,000 a year. This was where she met and worked with her future husband and business partner, Richard Ross, who was the company's Finance Director. The company boomed, and by 1982 she had doubled her salary and was opening a new outlet every six weeks. But Mirman and Ross were not happy about the pressure they were working under and became increasingly irritated by the demands which were being made by their boss.

At the time she had already put up the idea of a shop for hosiery

## The Unemployables

within Tie Rack, but it had been rejected because the business was expanding too fast. She and Ross decided to set up on their own and used their spare time to develop the idea and to trudge from bank to bank to try to get the backing. They had £1,000 each and were prepared to put up their flats as collateral, but they needed £45,000. They had no luck. 'I think it was basically down to the fact that most men didn't know anything about tights, so they couldn't see the opportunity. They could understand ties though, because they all wore them.' Eventually they found a backer, Barclays Bank, which promised to help them with the support of the Small Firms Loan Guarantee Scheme under which the government pays off 70 per cent of the debts if a firm goes bust, while the bank is responsible for 30 per cent.

In April 1983, the first Sock Shop opened in London. 'When we were running low on stock we used to cycle down to my mother's house to get some more stock in the basket.' Working from seven in the morning until nine at night, they exceeded the initial sales forecast three times over. With the success of the first store, they then went on to open up new outlets at other main-line stations. Throughout the eighties the business grew and grew and eventually went public in 1986. The pinnacle of this was when Mirman was voted Businesswoman of the Year in 1988. Then came the recession.

Sock Shop was one of the first high-profile companies to suffer when the recession began to bite. 'It was a combination of things. People tend to buy tights, etc., when the weather is cold. But we had a succession of mild winters and hot summers. We also tried to expand in the US and that was a real burden on the business. Then the interest rates went up. We could see the problems coming a long way off, and there was very little we could do about it.'

The final straw was the transport strikes, which closed the stations where Sock Shop had many of its outlets. 'The passing trade just dried up and a third of our shops were closed one day a week for fifteen weeks. That had an effect not only on the day of the strike, but on the day before and after, because travel was disrupted because of the rolling stock being in the wrong place, etc. It was a complete disaster, and there was nothing we could do about it.'

'The one thing I learnt from this was "Don't get into debt". It was just a relief when the whole thing was laid to rest.' The company was put into the hands of the receiver and sold on to venture capitalists who refinanced it. Sock Shop is still trading profitably now, but without the two founders.

It was natural instinct for Mirman to set up again and recently she came up with a new idea. She says starting another business in the wake of Sock Shop was 'quite frightening, but once it got going it was a tremendous boost to the system'. Trotters is the name of the new shop and its central character is Dunwoody N. Trotter, a pig, because 'pigs on socks and tights were always a best seller at Sock Shop. It also had to have an appealing image for adults, as well as kids, to look at.'

The key to success for Mirman is looking around in your everyday life for people who are having problems that you could potentially help them out of. Her own problem was taking her children shopping: 'There was nowhere I could go to get children's shoes where it was easy, convenient and comfortable. There was nothing to entertain them. There was the same problem with having children's hair cut.' Instead of bemoaning the fact, she and her husband went out and set them up. Whatever her reservations may have been about the new venture, they were completely dispelled by the queue outside the front door on the first day.

Is the intention to build the store into another chain to rival Sock Shop? 'Absolutely not; we would ideally like three shops, that's all. This time we want to enjoy it. The whole environment has changed. The eighties were about expanding and getting bigger, now we've moved on.'

A lot of thought has gone into the shop – for instance, to keep children still long enough for their hair to be cut, she sits them in front of a fish tank. 'The parents are then free to wander around the store and they often use the time to buy other things. Because the atmosphere is fun and relaxing, it attracts children and parents. It's friendly but still very professional because selling hairdressing and shoes means the staff do have to be well-trained.'

Mirman believes her own success is down to leading by example. She never asks any of her staff to do something she would not do. At present, both she and Ross can be found personally ministering to customers every day of the week. 'My husband is also an important factor. Husband and wife teams can either work very well or they can be a terrific disaster, but it works if you have different personalities which are complementary. Richard's very good at the financial side and I do all the merchandising. He's a real pessimist and I'm an optimist so we tend to balance each other out.' Another important factor is how she views the lucky breaks she has had: 'The difference is whether you are capable of taking your chances. We are all presented with them.'

In her spare time, such as there is, she rides, plays tennis or swims, but if she has more time she takes the dog out. On longer periods she will go to France to see her family, who are an important source of inspiration for her. The principles that Mirman abides by were passed down by her mother and will be passed on down to her own daughter who, she says proudly, recently asked if she could earn some money by cleaning the car. If she also turns out like her mother, she may be one to watch.

## David Northrop – Waiter to Bond Dealer (And Back)

David Northrop sounds a bit like Harry Enfield's character 'Loadsamoney', and he has in fact made quite a bit of money. But there the similarity ends. By contrast to the East End plasterer, Northrop is bright, polite, charitable and understated. He does not even want to 'wave his wad'.

He was born in a hotel, brought up in one and later learned to manage one. But a lot happened in the meantime. 'I hated school and left it as soon as I could at sixteen. Naturally enough, I worked in a hotel as a waiter and then went to catering college part-time to learn a bit more,' he says. He progressed to a hotel in London and got involved in outside catering.

One day he was working in a hospitality tent at a 'posh do', when a group of City bond dealers came in. He started talking to one who told him he'd make a good bond dealer. Characteristically, he took the offer seriously and had a go. It was the classic City rags-to-riches story. Northrop made his fortune, buying and selling bond futures. 'It was quite easy. Once you understood the jargon, it was just like selling anything else. It taught me about life, it taught me about the City. I made some money out of it and bought a flat, but I could see the recession coming, so I thought I'd better get out.'

Northrop's maturity is well beyond his years: 'My hotel job taught me a trade (he can cook and wait tables). My City job taught me about business. My estate agent's job taught me about negotiating and now I bring all this together in my current job. But it doesn't matter what you do – it's the approach that counts. When I left the City, I went to work briefly for a mate of mine who ran an estate agents called Winkworths in London. I sold that much property I became the top salesman out of 54 offices in London. I just did what the others would do – that is give a good service. I was selling a property a day and that was in the recession.'

From there he developed many contacts, one of which was setting up a hotel and equestrian centre in Sussex. He went fifty-fifty with his partner and built Crockstead Farm Hotel. Northrop was responsible for designing, building and setting the whole place up. 'I didn't know anything about that sort of thing, but I picked it up as I went along. I was worried sick about everything.'

It seems Northrop learns fast. He went to a hotel exhibition and got three quotes for everything. 'That way I found out what the right cost should be. I bought everything, carpets, curtains, floor tiles, kitchen equipment – everything.' Northrop frankly admits that he didn't tell anyone how little he really knew about building: 'But you know what they say: "until you make it – fake it".'

There is nothing fake about David Northrop. He is the real McCoy. He does what he says he will, and plays to win. One of the things he did while the restaurant was being built was to work as a part-time waiter in the nearest competitive hotel. 'When we started Crockstead I took every client from the other hotel. They thought it was a bit odd me just being a waiter, but I really enjoyed it. It was researching the competition at first hand.'

The business accelerated very quickly, largely due to Northrop's approach. 'Word of mouth is really important. For instance, I adopted a local charity. I raised some money for them, and they gave out some of my leaflets in return. I always look for organisations that can be of mutual assistance. I even go out and knock on doors to meet people. People are too shy in this country, especially my age. You know they just can't be bothered to make the effort. That's what it's really about. I could stand up and speak about making the effort, I feel that strongly about it.'

Apart from knocking on doors to drum up business, he also organised theme evenings to boost trade. He held veteran car weekends, Chinese evenings, gliding and romantic weekends. As soon as anyone expressed an interest, Northrop was there with a quote. Not surprisingly in its first year his restaurant and hotel turned over £400,000 a year.

His next venture was typically enterprising – organising trips to Britain for Russians. He takes them around all the sights of London and the City and gets British businessmen to talk to them. He has even made the effort to learn Russian so he can talk to them more easily. 'They came to stay at the hotel one weekend as a party and as a gesture of goodwill I gave them a bottle of wine each. That's how the whole thing started,' he says.

Now it is up and running, he is optimistic. 'I'm convinced I'll be a millionaire by the time I'm forty-five. It's pretty straightforward – every quarter I write out goals. I can show you my goals for the next year. You have to say "I will save this" or "I will achieve this". I will buy a Porsche by the end of the year. I will do it. You also have to break the goals down. People used to laugh at me at school. Even my parents used to laugh, but I think they know different now.'

'You have to make the effort. It doesn't matter what you do. It's the way you look at things. If I was a dustman, I'd buy the company and go private. It was exactly the same when I was doing estate agency. I used to say to people "I'll show you this property at anytime you want. Two in the morning if necessary." I showed a property at 11.00 pm and sold it. I used to work Sunday afternoons as well. Let's face it, that's when people have time to look. I did think estate agents lied too much, however. I used to say to people "That's no good" or "That's a nice property" and only sold what I thought were good properties.'

Ultimately, when he's made his fortune, he says he will retire and make another fortune for charity. 'I'm not really the retiring type, so I'd probably want to keep going, but with another objective.'

Needless to say, Northrop has a lot of energy. Eighteen-hour days are standard. His staff complain that he wears them out. 'It's annoying sometimes when people run out of energy, but I have to learn to accept people for what they are.'

If anyone needed a formula for success, they could hardly do worse than follow his lead: 'It's all about being honest and working hard. I'm convinced that's the case. If you work at it, you will do well. I get a real buzz out of doing something well. I want to make a fortune for me and then do the same thing for charity; then I wanna be on Wogan!' The way things are going for him, Wogan may end up being on Northrop.

## Bruce Oldfield – No Problems, Only Opportunities

Those who make excuses about not succeeding should look carefully at Bruce Oldfield. On the face of it, a glamorous, well-connected, media celebrity fashion designer, but Bruce Oldfield was an adopted black child brought up in a Barnardo's home in the North of England. He had everything against him, his background, his upbringing, his locations, some would even say his colour. Yet Oldfield treats it all as if success were simplicity itself: ' You just decide what you want and go for it.' But that hides a tenacity, ambition and sheer talent that is not immediately apparent.

Oldfield's secret is that he has taken all these disadvantages and turned them to his favour. His Northern upbringing has contributed to the grit and the 'feet on the ground' approach. His lack of family has allowed him not to be pigeonholed or stereotyped. With his growing status, it also became part of the mystery behind the legend. He is seen in the company of other successful people, because he is likeable. As they say, it takes genius to recognise genius.

Looking back on his rise Oldfield is matter-of-fact: 'I'm only in Chelsea because I have to be here – I was brought up in the North-East and in Sheffield. You could never do what I do in the North, but perhaps now that's different. I moved down here in 1971 working in a house someone lent to me – it was ramshackle and I slept and worked in one room.'

Oldfield glosses over his childhood as if it were of no interest. Some years ago he actually got to see his files from the Barnardo's children's home. In 1957, there was a letter that said: 'The child's foster-mother believes he will be a fashion designer.' This was an incredible prediction. 'I had wanted to be in fashion from the age of fifteen but everyone said: "Nay lad, get your A levels first." So I did, and I was going to go to Leeds Fashion School, but I didn't get good enough grades. Instead, I went to teacher training college, which was good for my confidence. I lost weight, grew taller and started to get all the girls.'

That's when things really started moving for Oldfield. 'I'd lived all my life as an orphan up till then and that, allied with the Northern upbringing and temperament, is very useful. It serves you in good stead later on. It keeps your feet on the ground. I shoot straight from the shoulder and tell it how it is. Being straight is very important.'

He says that not having any family to fall back on was a positive advantage in some ways, 'because it enabled me to move among a wide circle of friends, all the way from royalty downwards. I think it's essential to be adaptable.' He learnt his skills at a very young age and could knit, sew and weave before he was ten. 'It was very much if you want something, you make it yourself, because buying it was out of the question.'

Does he now find it difficult to relate to people who don't come from that background? 'No. Where you are is not as important as where you're going.' This is an understatement from one who chats as easily to the postman as he does to the Princess of Wales. Oldfield says that he is more intimidated by the higher echelons of fashion than with other famous people.

'They are, after all, just people. If you think you can do something, then go for it. One of the most common things that was said to me was, "Who do you think you are?", and it used to get right up my nose. You don't have to be arrogant, just know your own mind. People's expectations of life, especially from my background, are fairly low, so it's up to you to raise them, nobody will do it for you. I really thought well, hell, I wanted to be successful at something, and the only thing I could do was fashion. When people ask me what I could have done besides fashion there's nothing I can think of – there's nothing I'd really rather do.'

When he first came to London, he set his sights on going to St Martin's College of Art. 'I applied to them and they said they wouldn't take me, so I just took my portfolio along there and grabbed the principal every time she left her office. Eventually she said I could be admitted to the college, but after six months I decided it wasn't for me. I'd been offered the chance to do a range of promotions for Revlon when they launched Charlie in this country. They paid for the clothes and I had already enough examples to complete the course so I left the college. At that year's show, my clothes were the opening exhibit and I got a lot of press from it.'

What sort of problems has he encountered since? 'I'm sure there has been colour prejudice, but once you get to a certain stage in your career, celebrity status overrides everything. It's almost as if fame compensates for anything.'

The other main problem he still has is that people don't take him seriously. 'Part of the problem of being in fashion is that people perceive you as being a rather foppish or silly character. I've had to have a go at people who are patronising in their attitude. First and

## The Unemployables

foremost I'm a designer, not a businessman, but people have some strange ideas of fashion. I'm not a creative genius, my clothes are not way out, they're classical. I take a practical approach to clothes, as I do to everything.'

There are also things that he dislikes about the fashion industry. 'I hate the transient side of fashion, but I can adapt my ideas and that's an important thing.' In the recession Oldfield made sure that demand continued by designing cheaper dresses. 'People are still getting quality and glamour. The trick is to be sexy without being vulgar. In its broadest sense, that's probably a good recipe for life.'

The other problem he has is being recognised in the street. 'The hardest thing to put up with is people coming up to you and saying "Bruce Oldfield – Tubular Bells – that's a great album!" Generally speaking, people are very nice and generous. You get good seats in restaurants and if you don't, you want to know why!'

Oldfield says that many people from the North end up doing very well because they keep a good perspective on things. 'The stardom can go to people's heads and that's when the Northern attitude is really useful. You never get above yourself, because you know that it's not real. Northerners tend to be quite realistic about what they can achieve, and develop a practical approach. You don't have to believe in all the hype, just in yourself, that's all.'

## Peter Parfitt – Laughing All The Way

With his ruddy complexion and schoolboy grin, Peter Parfitt's recipe for success is easy to spot. Enjoy what you do and you will excel at it naturally. He applied this philosophy as much when playing national and county cricket as he now does running his own corporate hospitality company.

Parfitt played cricket for Middlesex and England for many years before retiring in 1972 to a pub in Yorkshire, near to where he still lives with his wife, Jill. Making the transition from cricketer to businessman was not easy: 'I was lucky. I had some good advice and was helped by some nice people. Some others were not so lucky.' Parfitt says that many people come out of successful sporting careers thinking they can repeat their achievements in business. 'There's no doubt about it, if you have a name it's easier to meet people who can open doors for you, but the downside is that you are more gullible because you don't know the terrain and can attract unscrupulous people. Some sports stars will get money from a benefit game or a pension and put it into a business and there are a lot of people just waiting to take advantage.' It seems that if you are successful in one particular field, people also think you might be a soft touch. 'It's completely different outside of what you know. By the time I retired from cricket, I knew as little as someone who was starting out at the age of eighteen.'

Parfitt started out buying a pub working on the basis that, although he might mess the business up, he would always have the investment in the bricks and mortar. He hired himself a good manager and it went from strength to strength. The attraction of the place was that locals could come in and see Parfitt and his pals (Fred Truman, Bob Willis, Derek Underwood, etc.) at play. The customers got good food and beer, a convivial atmosphere and a chance to see big names pop in and stagger out.

He made sure that the business could run on its own, without him being involved. He could then do what he was good at, i.e. swashbuckle around the bar making ribald comments with the locals. This is all part of his success philosophy: 'Just be yourself and enjoy it.' Parfitt has some well-known friends but he has never lost the common touch. He is in his element in a social environment, as

## The Unemployables

happy swearing with locals as he is exchanging witticisms with celebrities.

It was this 'life-and-soul-of-the-party' approach that appealed to BT in 1979 when they asked him to lay on a 'bash' at Lord's for one of their clients. He invited a few of his old cricketing contacts to make it more entertaining. The following year BT asked him to do the same again and they were followed by Thorn EMI. From here the business expanded and it occurred to him that he should really start hosting the parties with his own company.

One of the problems with laying on entertainment at sports grounds is the physical limit of the ground's capacity. One day he was visiting Twickenham and was chatting away to the marketing manager about how to use the gaps between the stands. This set him thinking and he came up with the idea of a mobile structure which could be moved from event to event and fitted into gaps such as the one at Twickenham. But progress was slow and he had to visit all the major sporting events to persuade them to take up his idea. Eventually he ended up back at Twickenham. 'We got a contract from the Rugby Football Union for eighteen units which seated thirty apiece. They were supposed to go in and out after each game but they were such a success that they now go into position in early September and come out in May.' By doing this, he increased the club's capacity by 500-600 people a day in prime seats which earn the highest revenue.

Parfitt makes it all sound deceptively easy, but going from sport into business has been difficult: 'I have visible scars from the process, but I have learnt an enormous amount. Some people don't even last long enough to do that. I have a partner who's very good and helps me out quite a bit. I make as many contacts as I can – I'm good at meeting people in a social environment. I pick up business cards all the time. It's essential to talk to people in a relaxed, social atmosphere away from a formal pitch situation. If I am successful, it is because I have the nous to get other people to do the work I can't do, on my behalf. We've made at least £100,000 profit each year.'

This hides the fact that in the first two years of his business he managed to repay the £1.25m investment on his mobile equipment. 'We run a tight ship. We have a blinkered existence and we concentrate on our business. We don't keep going off at a tangent and take on the big boys.'

A lot of people might envy his lifestyle because it looks like he spends his time simply partying with all his friends. Behind the scenes there is a more serious Parfitt, one that pays attention to detail and quality of service. But the sense of humour is never far away.

Parfitt manages his people like they were a sports team. And people seem to work hard for him because they like him. Previous employees say that he is completely unstuffy and always ready for a joke. With nervous waiters on their first time out, he will walk up to them and say, 'When you're serving that old buffer, make sure you don't spill anything on him; he's very important and let me tell you, he's a right so-and-so.' The staff say it somehow makes things easier, because they do work with some well-known celebrities who can be condescending.

When he wants to drum up business, he writes to a list of 4,000 clients and when he gets enquiries he goes to see them personally to let the charm loose. This certainly worked with the BBC and now their TV crews commentate on matches at Wimbledon from a Parfitt box.

Is there any secret to the way he works? 'The trick is to think like your customer. If they're trying to sell to their customers, they want to get to know them and a cricket match is ideal. You know at some stage they will want to talk. It's no use inviting them to the North stand of Wembley Stadium during a Cup final.' This is central to the Parfitt proposition – put people together in convivial surroundings and leave them to sort out their business.

His latest idea is nostalgia weekends, where clients who once harboured ambitions to play football with Bobby Charlton or golf with Lee Trevino can get together with their childhood heroes. These give him the chance to combine business with pleasure because Parfitt is also a keen golfer. His other hobby is watching cricket: 'I never thought I'd enjoy watching cricket at a lower level than I played, but seeing my son play gives me immense pleasure.'

At the end of a hard day Parfitt is still having fun. His favourite announcement (in mock aristocratic voice) is that he's 'orf to the old matrimonial chariot'. This illustrates the last rule of Parfitt's policy – 'Leave 'em laughing.'

## Bob Payton – The Great American Dream Salesman

*Sadly, Bob Payton died in 1994. The author has left this live interview in the present tense.*

You can tell Bob Payton was constructed in the USA – like something from Detroit in the sixties, he is massively over-engineered with enormous body work which emits a low-down growl. He is a big man – over six foot and well built with it. Big men are supposed to be sluggish, but not this one. Perhaps it's something to do with the number of cans of coke he has for breakfast. He can't sit still for thirty seconds. His eyes are constantly darting around the room, betraying boredom at anything which demands slightly less than all his concentration. His word count is through the roof, as his mouth struggles vainly to keep up with his brain.

Payton is the man behind the My Kinda Town group of restaurants. Individually, these are chains like Henry J. Bean's, The Chicago Pizza Pie Factory, Chicago Meatpackers, etc. None are particularly big, but put together they form quite an empire.

He used to be an account executive with one of the largest American agencies in London and wanted a bit of a change. So in 1977 he opened The Chicago Pizza Pie Factory: 'I could never get a decent pizza in this town, so I thought I'll make 'em myself.' What motivated him to go out on his own? 'Freedom. It's a desire to do what you wanna do. I just had better ideas than the clients and I wanted to do it on my own. Now I get to do it all.'

With the success of one restaurant he opened another. Now his restaurants are all over the world, but he stays based in London, not because he particularly likes it – he misses America too much for that.

One of the things he doesn't like about the British is soccer. 'What's so good about twenty-two guys chasing a ball around?' he says, playing devil's advocate. Characteristically, he decided to import US grid iron football (just because he wants to watch it – or so he says) and has been organising matches and setting up teams. This has already proved highly popular. Payton says American

Football translates well because 'there are a growing number of people in this country who buy the American dream. They go and watch a match and they're there. They've got the baseball hat, the jersey, the hamburgers, the whole bit.'

Underneath the blustering exterior there is a man who is extremely sensitive to things going on around him. He is quick to recognise trends in the market place and he was doubly quick to recognise the onset of recession and trimmed his costs accordingly. Was he concerned about it? 'Hard times don't last forever – tough guys do. You must have the vision and the passion. It doesn't matter who the government is, or what the people say, you just have to get on and do it.'

Payton, it has to be said, is deliberately over the top; the caffeine in the Coke must be going full steam ahead by now. 'I set up the Pizza restaurants so I could get a good pizza here. Now I've got the best of both worlds. I can go fox-hunting with Lord and Lady Howsyourfather in the beautiful English countryside, then I can go and get a decent pizza. I got it all.' He says his behaviour is symbolic of global trends emerging: 'We are beginning to get the emergence of a one-world culture, which has parts of each in it, but where people live life to the full.'

It has to be said that Payton partly owes his success to the British; if they weren't such 'a nation of culinary heathens' he would not have been able to make an impact. This is something the portly American feels strongly about: 'There is absolutely no food culture here at all. If you go around the world in every city you will see Italian, French and American restaurants. No British. The street food here is the worst I've ever seen anywhere in the world. A girl came into one of my restaurants the other day – she had nachos and French fries – I thought she was gonna die of carbohydrate poisoning.'

Being heavily meat-orientated in his restaurants, does he see the rise of the vegetarian as a threat? 'No, it's not a lunatic fringe, but my chefs have instructions to produce good-tasting food with or without meat. The Americans have been eating more healthily than the Brits for a long time. You can go into a supermarket and buy low carbohydrate, diet, decaffeinated, sodium-free anything there.'

It is quite clear that Payton takes a close interest in the way his businesses are run, at a very detailed level. He checks everything. He has his own snagging lists. He is also particular about the way his staff work. Payton believes that people should not have job titles if they're being used as a way of defending their credibility. 'People shouldn't say "What do you do?", but "What do you want me to do?". "How can I help you?" is the most important thing to ask.'

## The Unemployables

This man's secret is obviously related to his level of energy. He is bright and very quick, but his staff probably feel that because he gives off so much enthusiasm, they should too. He is the sort of man who could power three cities when he's at work. Being around him is not so much of a buzz, more of a loud drone.

As with all great achievers, there are some facets to his character which understandably ruffle the feathers of the modest. For instance, he had his handwriting analysed recently and it said 'Not a great team member but a dynamic and creative leader', which according to Payton is 'about right'. He is brash. He is loud. But he is also good at what he does, so why shouldn't he say what he feels?

Perhaps it is ego that prompts when he is asked 'Who does he particularly admire?' and he says 'Nobody'. Aware of the fact this may sound arrogant, he quickly changes it to a more playful answer: 'Well my role model is Peter Pan. I liked Margaret Thatcher...she spoke the same language as me. I also like the work that Tom Peters does. He gives the sort of speech that I would give.'

Immediately after our interview, Payton was going to 'sort out' some of the members of his serving staff who had not been giving away a free guidebook as they were supposed to. When this man goes on the warpath, the cowboys call the cavalry. What followed promised to be living proof that the man who sells American dreams sells nightmares as well.

## Jozsef Pinter – Beating The Really Red Tape

Jozsef Pinter is an extraordinary combination of businessman, diplomat and navvy. A self-taught blacksmith, he built his business up from nothing to one of the most profitable operations in Hungary. He has the brains of a professor and the body of a labourer. His hands, which are like bunches of bananas, are as much at home on a lathe as they are on a personal computer.

He has become one of the shining examples of Eastern European capitalism. But it wasn't always that way. The communists hated him and tried for many years to close him down. They sent armies of government inspectors to check up on him and search his factory. He has been investigated 217 times by the state. It was all deliberate state policy. They discouraged free enterprise by drowning it in paperwork and regulations. They ranged from the government inspector of bicycles through to the sheep-dip officer. He did try to explain to the latter that he didn't have a sheep-dip because his factory made steel components, but the man wouldn't listen and turned the premises upside down looking for it. He eventually found what he was looking for, but they turned out to be acid baths. The chap who sold them to Pinter had accounted for them as sheep-dips to avoid government tax. Nevertheless Pinter was fined and inconvenienced severely.

Pinter was born in the small village of Kecel, one hundred miles South of Budapest, which is where he built his steelworks. He has become a local lad who is now internationally known. He will turn his hand to anything. Besides brake parts for Mercedes and General Motors (with whom he has signed a contract worth £4m), he also makes machine tools, generators for German tanks, parts for French missiles and refrigerators for the Russians. He has even made parts for an Austrian nuclear reactor.

The combination of engineering skill, versatility, low labour costs and bargaining power make the Pinter Steelworks highly profitable. His new plant cost £10m to build but it has paid for itself. Most of his profits are now reinvested in the latest technology – electron microscopes, special alloy forges and computer-aided design systems. He has also spent heavily on training. Out of a staff of five hundred, sixty-four are apprentices receiving a multi-disciplinary training in electronics, engineering and computer technology. 'You can't get quality work without training your staff,' he says.

No trade union or party representative is allowed in the factory because of his bitter experiences – '...It took us long enough to get rid of them. They contributed nothing. If I pay my people good money then they're happy.' There is no evidence of discontent: staff have clean restaurants, modern washing facilities and free buses from as far away as 100 km. His factory has an 'open shirt' policy and a relaxed, but disciplined air.

He says he wants to make Hungary great again. He is especially proud of the fact that Hungary helped to bring down the Berlin Wall. By opening their border with Austria, they allowed East Germans into the West for the first time, which gave the Russians no alternative but to open the wall.

The first national project he has lined up is the construction of a tower 150 metres tall. This is planned to be the central showpiece for the 1995 Budapest-Vienna Expo. It will be built by his own engineers and used for a combined telecommunications, radio and TV system which will replace Hungary's antiquated networks. It will cost £5m to build, which is one year's profit from his factory. He already has the 12 relevant telecommunications licences required by the state.

He met both the then President Bush and Prince Charles when they came to visit Hungary, and is keen to foster links with both America and England. 'If Western businessmen want to find out how to run a business, they should come here. I will show them,' he says.

He would also show them how to spend money. Pinter has taken readily to the life of a capitalist. He has a passion for expensive cars and light aeroplanes and is planning to build a runway adjacent to his factory to accommodate three of his own. He drives a Mercedes which, although common in the West, is regarded as the ultimate capitalist totem in Hungary. Native Lada drivers often risk life and limb to tell their friends that they actually overtook one. Unfortunately, the roads are frequently littered with little pieces of such cars which did not survive to bask in the glory.

Pinter has succeeded where others failed in Hungary because he never let himself get caught up in the chain of debt which links companies. Although he still buys his raw materials domestically, all of his customers are now based outside the country. He gets payment in Western currencies, which gives him bargaining power with his local suppliers. He says he can walk into a supplier's office and put an attaché case full of cash on the desk and get a delivery on any day he wants. With inflation running rampant, everybody wants Western cash because it holds its value.

Without the bureaucracy, Pinter feels unstoppable. 'Under the communists, I felt like I was carrying around two heavy suitcases. Now I feel like a sprinter.' He is now looking at other projects such as shopping malls, business parks and a national hotel chain. Now that the iron curtain has lifted, he is surprised that British businessmen are not more interested in Hungary. 'They think they're badly off with their red tape, they should have been here five years ago,' he says.

He says his success has partially been due to copying others. He used to travel to the West whenever he could, to study the way companies were run. This gave him a massive advantage over the local competition, which he describes as having stood still for forty years.

He admits there is still much to be done, but he is grateful to have the chance. Pinter thanks God and Gorbachev, in that order, for his wealth: 'If you're a capitalist, this is like the new Garden of Eden.'

In the centre of Budapest there is a square full of statues which stand testimony to Hungary's historic love of heroes. Sovereigns, statesmen and soldiers and, until recently, communist politicians, like Lenin, were all there. Mysteriously, Lenin's statue disappeared, never to return. The government diplomatically said it had been 'removed for cleaning'. Locals wondered why it had to be smashed into such tiny pieces for the cleaning to take place.

The people now prefer to idolise living capitalists as opposed to dead communists. Pinter repeatedly gets asked by the new government to go into politics and do for the country what he has done for his firm, but he is not interested: 'I don't like politics and I'm not ready to retire yet; maybe when I'm tired and old, I'll have a go. The thing about businessmen is that we understand each other. We don't have to talk in riddles.' It seems the politicians may have some time to wait.

## Fiona Price – Channelling The Energy

It's difficult to know where to start with Fiona Price. Successful businesswoman, Commonwealth Games athlete, accomplished horse rider, qualified faith healer, motivational guru, the list is endless.

A petite 5 ft. 4 in., she doesn't look strong enough to be an athlete. Then it becomes clear that here is a person whose strength lies not in her pectorals but in her personality. Like some organic storage heater, she radiates energy.

Her business is simple enough. She provides financial planning and consultancy, mainly for executive women. Her Covent Garden office in London accommodates eight other people who help her look after the one thousand clients she has accumulated in the last five years.

The only hint of the determination behind her soft spoken modesty is in the way she delivers her words – swiftly, confidently and precisely: 'All the way through my childhood, my parents had encouraged me to do my own thing. One of the most critical aspects of all is to be able to retain a perspective and to manage a large number of situations at any one time. You must also have a wide range of domestic as well as commercial goals.'

Price's father was a businessman and her mother was a housewife, but all the family were involved with business decisions. 'We were brought up with business being discussed over the dinner table. So it all seemed quite natural to me. My family are all high-achievers and encouraged me at every step. I just developed with the disposition that I would not take "No" for an answer.'

Her family background has been important for her self-development. 'You have to be prepared to go against the grain sometimes and the emotional and psychological support from my parents helped enormously. I always found it difficult to conform, basically because I never had a need to. You have to develop your confidence so you are not completely influenced by those around you. '

Although she was well educated, with a degree in psychology and an Master's in marketing, she says it was of no importance: 'The problem with education is that it is geared to big business. There is nothing which helps people start up on their own. My own education was really dovetailed to fit in with my rowing. The Master's degree combined with the sport was extremely demanding. I trained three hours a day and studied for seven. I was never academically confident – I was more interested in sport. The education was just an excuse.'

Despite being a strong team player, Price had her sights fixed firmly on being self-employed: 'It was clear to me that I was quite unemployable. I had my own ideas and wanted to be my own boss,' she says firmly. 'I had been frightened of maths all my life so I decided to challenge that. I started working with Financial Planning Services (FPS), where I was self-employed. I was allowed to use my own initiative and be independent and I really enjoyed it.'

The important thing about this environment for Price was the freedom and the responsibility: 'High-achievers get a real buzz from life, from new people, from new horizons, from new experiences and from stretching and developing themselves. The minute you think you've arrived you may as well curl up and die. Challenge is the food of life. This is not to be confused with those people who want to achieve to prove it to themselves. Eventually they have to cope with that as a problem. Real achievement involves being balanced and striving because you want to keep improving yourself and thereby being equipped to give to others. It's a never-ending experience.'

Even the bad days conform to this: 'Sometimes it is tough. Sometimes it is lonely. Sometimes you just want to crawl into a corner. But ultimately you have to believe in yourself and trust in your individuality. On the bad days, I wish I was in a big company where I had a fat salary. But that would be wrong for me because the problems are part of my challenge.'

Price used to have a partner in a business which broke up some years ago. 'It's probably true that you don't really know anyone until you've worked with them. I found that it ended up being a nightmare. If you want to succeed in business, you have to take responsibility and put 100 per cent in. If someone doesn't give their all, then you have to make that up if you really want to succeed, so you might as well be in business on your own.' The experience taught her a great deal about human nature: 'It's one thing to trust people to the stage you know they're honest and credible. But in business it's not enough; you have to see them at work and see how much they put in. When you're getting people to work for you, you have to be sure they have the right attitude and it's important to be very thorough. Nowadays I test people as to how they would approach certain tasks.'

Inevitably, if people want to succeed in business they have to start off small, and Price says that it has its own special requirements:

'What comes up again and again is that if you work for a small company you have to be prepared to put in much more because there are less people. The ones there are have to count. They have to be flexible and they have to be committed.'

She says women need specific qualities: 'They have to be more committed because there is more necessity to prove themselves. Personally, I don't think it's harder, but then again I'm used to it. There is no doubt that there is a "glass ceiling" for a lot of women. It's definitely there. Women who break through this, often at great personal sacrifice, must ensure that they leave the door open for others. They have to encourage company cultures to change. Women can be incredibly tenacious and tend to have a lot more stamina than men. They are also less into role playing.'

What is true from the performance of her business is that women with these qualities recognise them in her: 'People will come to us for one of a number of reasons. They may have a specific need for a pension or for an investment or whatever. Alternatively, they may want us to do a complete review of their finances to try and plan their future for them. The financial marketplace is so complex these days, so it's very important that people have continual access to us for professional and impartial advice.'

She says financial planning is not taken seriously enough: 'Just about everyone can benefit from it. People seem to think they have no money and therefore don't manage it and this becomes self-fulfilling. They don't manage their money, so they never have any to spare.' And this is especially true for high-achieving women: 'It's very important for women to be financially independent, because we live in times of very high divorce rates and job uncertainty. Financial independence can remove a lot of stress.'

It all seems to work. And so does she – 25 hours a day – even when she's riding she's thinking about other aspects of the business. Her early success has been meteoric.

Price's cuttings file already has more column-inches than Nelson. But if she is quietly proud of her success, it does not come out in ostentatious displays of wealth. She drives a modest car and lives in the countryside outside London. She rides frequently, and takes her holidays in North Wales. In her 'spare' time she is working on a book, which will be about people's relationship with themselves, because 'It's the most important relationship you can have. And it dictates whether you will be successful or not and how you relate to others. It's not so much how you get on with others, because if your relationship with yourself is a success then inevitably you will be with others. People have to learn to train their minds if they really want to succeed. They have to believe it. They have to want it. And they have to learn how. If they do, they will succeed.'

Fiona Price will be much bigger than financial planning because there are too many other things she wants to do. She wants to write more, and wants to help other people to achieve their full potential. Part of this is illustrated by her pursuit of faith healing. This is not done for commercial reasons. It just helps her to maintain her own health and it illustrates an essential truth in her life: 'It's simply about learning to channel your energy. There's nothing mysterious about it.'

## Matthew Stockford – Captain Fantastic

You don't get many real live superheroes these days. Of course, there are people who do remarkable things, but not many whose very day-to-day existence is an achievement.

All achievers have problems from time to time, because real success never comes easily. So what would stop you achieving your goals? A bit of snow? A cold? A sprained ankle? A broken leg? How about a broken back? The reason most people don't achieve their dreams is because something gets in their way. Over, under, around, through – people who succeed get past these problems somehow. What separates them all is how easily they give up. Some people like Matthew Stockford just don't.

It is almost tempting not to mention the fact that Stockford is paralysed from the chest down from a skiing accident, because it makes little or no difference to the way he lives his life. He drives a car, he works in an office, he careers downhill at sixty plus miles an hour....

Stockford started out skiing at the age of four on the slopes around his Cumbrian home. He went on to win the Cumbrian all-schools championship and represent his country at schoolboy level. At seventeen, out skiing with his brother in Italy, he suffered a high-speed fall and broke his back. 'It was just one of those things. I could have got a few bruises and skied on. As it was, I fell awkwardly and broke my back. Of course when I realised what had happened, I was very depressed, but I was surprised how easily I coped. I have tried not to let it change my life,' he says in a matter-of-fact way. This has to be an understatement to rank up there with Captain Oates' 'I'm going outside. I may be some time.'

Stockford has tried. And Stockford has succeeded. He has even turned it to his advantage: 'I am allowed to park my car in the executive car park, which is a perk that only the really important people have. And I'll tell you those nurses in hospital...'

Courtesy is one hallmark of real achievement and Stockford is always opening doors for people and saying 'Hello' as he wheels briskly down the corridor. He has the sort of joie-de-vivre that makes people glow as if they were sitting by a large fire.

Modesty is another of Stockford's hallmarks. He plays down all mentions of his disability: 'People treat me just like any other person, because I am. I often forget about the wheelchair.'

What would devastate some people, he treats as a minor inconvenience. 'If you see things as a problem, then they are. I just couldn't allow myself to think any differently. Anyway, logically I was stuck with it. There's nothing I can do, so I may as well get on with it. The only minor irritant is that people treat you differently, but they soon learn how.' Although there is nothing Stockford cannot do for himself, he occasionally asks for help – financial help to go hurtling down mountainside locked into his own skiing bobsleigh.

As you may have guessed, a mere accident did nothing to dampen Stockford's passion for skiing. Recovering in a spinal injuries hospital in Southport he vowed he would ski again: 'They did think I was mad, but then there wasn't much left to break!' A year later he was skiing downhill again at sixty miles an hour in a specially converted ski-bob. What's more, after this he went on to do his A levels and a degree and become a professional at one of the top surveying companies in London. Today he is still an award-winning downhill skier in his spare time and a professional surveyor by day.

Not surprisingly, Stockford is a goal-setter. He believes he will be an able-bodied skier again someday because of the progress being made in spinal injury treatment. 'That's something which will be incredible for me, it will give me a chance to compete on equal terms with my brother again.' This is goal number one: to beat his brother, who is also an accomplished skier. Goal number two is to walk and ski normally again.

His parents have been very supportive and provide not only help and motivation, but challenge in the shape of his elder brother, Andrew. 'There has always been a competitive edge between us and I was racing against him when I had my fall.'

Stockford is the only Briton ever to have represented his country in able-bodied and disabled disciplines. He skies in a chair fixed onto a single ski, a device which was designed by engineer and friend Alan Clark. 'Alan is a real stickler for detail. He just won't give up. He keeps stripping down the bob every five minutes to see if he can improve it.' (Apparently Stockford keeps wearing the chairs out, because Clark is always having to rebuild them after the hammering they get.)

Ironically the only thing that could slow Stockford down in the future is a lack of money. Sponsorship money is tight at the moment, although his employers, Jones Lang Wootton, give him some cash and time off work. Some ski sponsors have said that they consider him and other disabled people unsuitable for their product image.

## The Unemployables

Well if Stockford is unsuitable they should stuff their 'product image' and start talking to real people, because this man is an inspiration. The average ski-buyer would be proud to use a product endorsed by such a gutsy character. The narcissistic manufacturers should be reminded that experienced and professional world-class skiers do not use second-rate equipment, and that by implication anything Stockford uses has to be of Olympic standard. He is perfect investment material: his achievements are featured by national and international media and he has a strong personal following.

Those who make excuses for not achieving their goals should study Matthew Stockford well. Nothing slows him down. Nothing gets in his way. He has a thick skin and tons of physical strength.

He is an outstanding example of achievement, not to mention a fantastic skier. But first and foremost he is a fantastic person.

## Alan Sugar – Sweet and Sour

Alan Sugar is living proof that ordinary people can make it to the top. He came from a Polish-Jewish family in the East End of London and his surname is an anglicised version of Zuckermann. His style every bit reflects the combination of thrift and aggression which characterised his early youth.

The youngest of three children, as a boy he was remembered for always shouting and making a noise. This did not foretell his later character, which was quiet to the point of being remote. Later, in numerous jobs he was to hold, he lost the shyness but none of the thrift.

By the time he left school at 16, he had experience of selling all sorts of things, but his next move was into the Civil Service. This was as a result of parental pressure, seeing it as a chance of getting a 'good job'. A year later he was bored and took to selling reconditioned TV's from his mother's flat. He enjoyed this so much he packed in his job and took a full-time job selling tape recorders. In his travels he was to spot his first opportunity in the audio business, making plastic covers for stereos by undercutting the current supplier. Eventually he was to do this full-time, setting the company up as Amstrad (Alan Michael Sugar Trading).

His whole business philosophy has been analysed time and again, but it is essentially very simple. Work out what people want, produce it cheaper than anyone else and then sell it. If you get the first two right, the last does itself.

Of course, this is an oversimplification. Just working out what people want is not easy. Sugar used gut-feel for that in the early stages. Working in the stereo business Sugar soon discovered that the only difference between the various machines was the packaging. He knew the components were identical, so he decided build his own machines that gave the customer the product they wanted – low price, flashing lights and a highly technical looking design.

His music centres sold like hot cakes. Because they looked good, they seemed to sound good. He later applied this principle to computers, producing games machines that looked every bit like their larger cousins. At the heart of this was the ability to reduce the price by selling in quantity. 'Anticipating mass trends is what we are about;

if something can be reproduced cheaply and in volume, we'll have a go,' he says.

Sugar is no genius. All of what he does is common sense, but then that commodity is often in short supply. He has learnt a few clever techniques, though.

Although he is a self-made man, there is no evidence that he worships his creator. His staff do that for him. 'His bark his worse than his bite, but you do get the feeling that if he did bite it would be well-nigh fatal,' says one of Sugar's management team. They have been called 'Sugar Lumps'; partly this is a reference to the sort of personal loyalty that Sugar inspires and partly because of the uncanny physical similarity between them (curly hair, close cropped beards, East London backgrounds, etc.). It seems Sugar likes to surround himself with people from similar backgrounds, hands-on, down-to-earth types who are not afraid to roll their sleeves up.

Getting respect from people is important to Sugar. It is said that when people first come to work for him, he virtually ignores them for the first three months. New employees get to the point where nothing they do will impress him. Then one day he says 'Hello', and they think the world of him. It is a deliberate process.

He also puts a similar psychological pressure on his customers. When trying to get products into a store, he has been known to get family members to phone up and constantly ask for Amstrad products until the owner of the store calls him back. Sugar used this strategy time and again for getting into some of the largest retailers in the country.

He is very good at understanding what people's greatest fears are, and using them to get what he wants. People often build up an impression of him which is totally false, but which has been entirely engineered by Sugar himself.

The other thing he does well is to concentrate on the important things. For instance, he once turned down giving a lecture at the prestigious Harvard Business School because he didn't think he could teach them anything. 'Anyone who talks five-year plans, talks crap,' he says bluntly. Sugar means that to be a true opportunist you have to be able to react quickly to the environment, irrespective of whether it conforms to your plans. The other secret to Sugar's success is having interests outside of the business. He is a tennis fanatic, playing regularly on the courts in his garden at home. He says he particularly admires Ivan Lendl's cold, calculating style.

He also learnt to fly and used to pilot his own planes around Europe. One day things went wrong. 'It didn't sound right when I landed but when I took off it really went bang,' he says of the time his engine failed. The offending piston is still on his desk. His wife, Ann, put her foot down and insisted that he use more orthodox transport. This sort of exploit has added to the folklore surrounding Sugar.

His family philosophy is also simple. Look after them as they looked after you and keep yourself to yourself. He applies to this to his parents and his three children.

Sugar says the thing which marks him out from his peers is an ability to learn from his mistakes, albeit the hard way. This ability, he says, will take him to the top, where he intends to stay.

## David Sullivan – Press On

OK, so the business is sex, but who's being moralistic about this? David Sullivan has been very successful in the business of publishing. Some of it has been pornographic, some of it has been scandal sheets, but he has been successful in quite 'legitimate' businesses. He is a racehorse owner and the owner of Birmingham City Football Club. He owns a stud farm and several brood mares.

Sullivan was born into a working-class background in Cardiff in 1949, where he says his early role models were football players and boxers. But he was bright and progressed to Queen Mary's College, London, where he gained an honours degree in economics.

His early career was in advertising but he soon set up his own mail order business, which was followed by the launch of the first in a string of soft-porn magazines, before going into newspapers in 1986.

'I admire Rupert Murdoch now,' he says. Clearly, his ambitions and models have changed, but then that's what you'd expect from a man who has already achieved his lifetime's goal – to be a millionaire – at the age of 24. Although he got what he wanted, he says that his greatest achievements are still to come. This is going to be a difficult enough task, seeing what he has done already.

David Sullivan is the man behind the *Sunday Sport*. This was the paper that brought you stories like: 'World War Two bomber found on moon' and 'Elvis found alive working in chip shop in Peckham'. Laughable, but highly successful. The paper now sells sixty million copies a year. What's more, this was done without any TV advertising at all, an incredible modern marketing achievement.

Whatever his achievements, Sullivan, behind his show biz brashness, says the principles are quite simple: 'My advice to people setting up in business now would be to do it part-time and test it first if you can.' But he is aware that it is not easy: 'I do not think success is encouraged in the UK.'

Sullivan believes his success is simply down to three qualities: 'Persistence, perseverance and hard work.' These are modest skills, given his talent for self-publicity and opportunism.

Perhaps the best way of summing up the essence of David Sullivan is in the following, supplied by him:

*Press on*
Nothing in the world can take the place of
Perseverance
Talent will not:
Nothing is more common than
unsuccessful men with talent.
Genius will not;
Unrewarded genius is almost a proverb.
Education alone will not;
The world is full of educated derelicts.
*Perseverance and determination* alone
are omnipotent.

## Sir Marc Weinberg – The Barrister-Salesman

Sir Marc Weinberg started out as a barrister in South Africa, but he wanted to broaden his experience so he came to Britain to do an English degree. It was to change his life. 'When I went back to South Africa there were people saying, "Oh you poor chap, not being at the Bar. It must be sordid to be in business." That's when I first realised that there was a terrific amount of snobbery among the professions about business. I realised that every group of people lives in a little black box and wonder what it's like outside. It's the same in many walks of life.'

Weinberg says it is easy to become a prisoner of your own circle of colleagues: 'If you look at law from the outside, it's just shuffling little pieces of paper around.' He therefore decided not to continue with it, and to find a different job: 'It never really entered my mind to go and work for anyone else in the long term.'

Funnily enough he does not regret any of his legal training. 'It's one of the finest trainings you can get. Whatever you do in business you will come up against regulations, tax laws, etc. Instead of having to sit down with three different people to create a product, I can manage pretty much on my own. My knowledge of law enables me to short-circuit the process. Legal training also helps structure the way you think. It all consists of arguing two sides – the upside and the downside. You get used to having this internal debate. I recommend anyone who wants to go into business to do legal training.'

He believes being a barrister is very similar to being a salesman. 'In the courtroom you're selling an idea to a judge and jury. Just like outside, when you're selling to people you have to persuade them. You have to get inside their minds. You won't win them over by proving you've got finer logic than they have or by proving them wrong – they will just get annoyed. You do it by understanding how they think, and persuade them that the way you think is in their interest as well. It's the same in law. If the barrister destroys his counterpart and makes him look a fool, the judge will not feel well disposed to him. You have to be more subtle.'

He also believes in getting the right mental attitude, which he applied when he founded Abbey Life Insurance: 'It's very important to have a positive approach to problems. You have to say I'm starting this and I'm going to succeed. I'm not wildly overconfident as a person – but it never entered my mind that Abbey Life wouldn't succeed.'

Although Weinberg started in business on his own at 28, he does not believe that people should start in business on their own as soon as they can. 'Do it as soon as you are able, but not as soon as you can. You've got to have a wide range of skills before you take on a project yourself. Somebody recently came to me who was very bright and had a glittering university record and wanted to start up on his own. I tried to persuade him not to. He had no experience of stubbing his toe, getting people to follow him or making decisions. The experience of what goes wrong when you're in or near the driving seat is invaluable. I had five years of legal practice where I saw a lot of things that went wrong.'

Weinberg already had some experience in the insurance business before he started Abbey Life in 1962: 'I had been doing a lot of work for a newly-formed South African insurance company, Liberty Life, and they asked me to start a branch in London for them. I said it made no sense to open a branch of a South African insurance company but, if they put up part of the money, I would start a new one.'

He says one of the first things he learnt was about categorising people: 'You soon learn there are different types of people. There are marketing types and administrative types, and the two don't mix well. They might get on, but they are not good at working together. This shows that there isn't necessarily a link between intelligence and success. It is important to be able to think analytically, but it's also important to be able to learn. One of the chaps I have worked with is Mike Wilson, who was Chief Executive of Allied Dunbar. He jokes about the fact that he's only got two or three O levels, but I don't know anyone who learns quicker about real world problems. He organises himself well, and he's fundamentally very intelligent although he doesn't have academic qualifications.'

Abbey Life succeeded in breaking the mould of other insurance companies at the time. 'One factor was that we were a small marketing-led company in an industry which was then largely bureaucratic. Before I started Abbey Life I walked around some of the City companies and said I wanted to take out an insurance policy. All the forms I received were full of jargon and very difficult to follow.'

Trying to gain more experience, he did a week's introductory course at Legal and General: 'At the end of the course they said they would show us the sales and marketing operation. We went down to this room where a chap told us that they tried to send a letter to one of their reps every year. I was appalled how little support they gave their staff.'

In theory, there was no reason why a client should take out a policy with a new company like Abbey Life, because other companies were more secure and better known. 'We made progress, but it was slow so I solicited a take-over from the American company ITT, and then we went forward in leaps and bounds. It became clear that I'd been in a big company's business with a small company's resources. After the merger we had the advantage of lots of resources and a very efficient structure with no bureaucracy. Our contact with clients was close. That's why Mike Wilson was so good. Until recently he had a direct line on his desk so that any of his sales people could call him and get help.'

With the backing of Hambros Bank, Weinberg left Abbey Life in 1970 and went on to start Hambro Life Assurance in 1971 (now called Allied Dunbar Assurance), which has become the largest unit-linked assurance company in the UK. He resigned as Chairman of Allied Dunbar in 1990 and became Executive Chairman of St James Place Capital plc, the parent company of the J. Rothschild Group, as well as Chairman of the recently-formed J. Rothschild Assurance.

For J. Rothschild Assurance he has drawn on his experience at Abbey Life. For instance, he contracted out all the administration work to Scottish Amicable. Even the investment team has been contracted out. He has only 25 backroom people as an overhead. 'You have to say to yourself: what is your great strength? Where am I better than anyone else? That's what we did and that's why we try to concentrate our effort on selling to people.' Although this sounds like Tom Peters, Weinberg does not stand by any management guru. He admires different people for different qualities – e.g. Arnold Weinstock for his leadership, John Sainsbury's eye for detail – and he has a 'sneaking admiration for Richard Branson – he's a great self-publicist'.

The only management technique Weinberg does have enthusiasm for is psychological testing. 'Possibly the most important thing you can do in business is to get good people around you. When you're doing a lot of recruiting, most interviews develop into mutual sales operations. The company is trying to sell itself to the employee and vice versa. I learnt to do a relatively simple psychological test which separated people into different categories. It was accurate enough for me to focus in on the most important aspects of character. It just warns me what to look for and short-circuits a process of getting to know somebody, which may take days.' He believes that once you know what types of people you're working with, it makes them a lot easier to manage. 'Some people love selling, some love precision, some love variety, some love routine. It enables me to slot round pegs into round holes. I still use it today – it's called a Cleaver test. It just helps me understand people.'

These days Weinberg spends a lot of his time doing charity work. Recently he got involved in the 'Percent Club' – where companies give a percentage of their profits to charity. He has marketed the idea in the same way as he marketed life insurance: 'You have to think of all the reasons people would have for saying "No" and have answers ready. We treat it as a serious business operation and it's tremendously satisfying.'

The other major satisfaction is his family life. 'They can be important because they're tremendously supportive. Alternatively, people succeed because they haven't got a family. I would never sacrifice family for business.'

Weinberg says there are no short cuts to success. 'This picture of the successful businessman having good contacts and just phoning up a few people to get it to work is just not true. It's not the way Arnold Weinstock works, it's not the way John Sainsbury works and I'm sure there aren't many who do that. A lot of success is due to hard work and detail.' He always leaves it at the office, however: 'I am interested to the point of obsession with computers, but mainly I like pottering around on boats, going skiing, seeing friends or being with my family.'

## Andrew Wilson and Tim Wilkinson – The Men With a Drink Problem

Andrew Wilson and Tim Wilkinson have a drink problem. They get through hundreds of bottles of champagne a month. Well, they do say that whatever you decide to do in life, it's essential that you enjoy it because those who really enjoy what they do become good at it and those that become good at what they do make money. The formula for success is as complex as that. But these guys don't drink it so much as sell it. They personalise bottles of champagne for companies and they love it (well who wouldn't?).

When you set out on this course you know that initially you will not have a great deal of money. But as you get better the money comes. This is the stage that Andrew Wilson and Tim Wilkinson are at. They are two young graduates who decided to go it alone, refusing to join the ranks of ex-public schoolboys in the City or be swallowed up by a large corporation. What they have achieved takes a lot more than a business degree, a rolled umbrella and a bowler hat. It takes drive, ambition and the willingness to take a risk.

When most other British students were quaffing pints of beer they were drinking champagne in Rheims, centre of the French champagne region and the town where they both went to college. And now, when their friends are sitting in front of computer screens in the City or kicking their heels in dole queues, these two are working for themselves. Within a year of graduating, both only 24-years-old, the pair had established their own import-export agency between Britain and France selling personalised champagne to blue chip companies. Not only that, but a few years later their company, Liquid ID Ltd, is a success.

So why start a company with champagne as a product when the country was in a recession? They both saw the opportunity, believed in it and the thought of failure did not even enter their heads. 'It really started when I first provided champagne for a ball at Oxford,' says Wilkinson, the French-speaking half of the two. 'The order was for seventy cases so I scraped together enough to finance it, borrowed a van and collected the champagne. Clearing it through customs was an invaluable lesson because I learnt how complicated it was.' The venture turned out to be the first success of many. 'It was then that I met Andrew and we decided to start doing more of it.'

The timing of the partnership formation was perfect for Wilson. Six months out of college he was looking out for an opportunity and jumped at the chance. Surprisingly, although they had both been at the same college for a year, they had not met before: 'I had always wanted to set up myself,' says Wilson. 'This was an opportunity that was staring me in the face.' It seemed a lot more appealing than sitting in front of a computer screen.

The thing that got them both off the ground was a £5,000 loan from the Prince's Youth Business Trust. They initially started wholesaling champagne to restaurants but realised very quickly that they could only make a low profit on it, so they targeted the big corporate accounts, including American Express, and moved up from there. The loan has been paid off and they are now considering expanding.

It isn't surprising that Wilson cites Richard Branson as an influence.

Wilkinson's influence came from his time in France – 'I drank so much champagne when I lived there that this was the only way to maintain the habit,' he confesses. Unfortunately, running his own company now leaves him with little time to consume the bubbly. The personal investment comes first: 'We don't lead a life of leisure. It's nice being in charge but we are also responsible for all the decisions. If you make a mistake you learn a lesson.'

It all sounds easy, but then the best people often make it sound so. Their success didn't come without a fight: 'The biggest problem with a small business is having the money to get started. Anything that helps with the bank is an advantage and I don't think that the bank would have even considered us if we had not been to college,' says Wilson. He points out that the Prince's Youth Business Trust backed them when others wouldn't.

The success has also taken a lot of persistence. When things have looked depleted in the champagne business the partners have developed into the packaging side; when mistakes have been made, they have learnt from them, but above all they have never given up.

'We take a risk just by being here. To be frank, a large majority of people's aspirations are to set up their own business, but they often haven't got the guts to do it,' says Wilkinson. Those who have are often not encouraged by large companies because others might see them as a challenge to their authority.

Nowadays there doesn't seem to be any reason why these two should think of wanting to work for anyone else. 'We are a very good team,' says Wilkinson. 'We both have our own area of the business to work in: Andrew looks after the finance and accounting side, and I look after the business with France. It's essential to have our own areas of expertise otherwise we would end up duplicating each other's efforts.'

The trick is to get organised and find your niche: 'We are only marketable to a small amount of people,' Wilson adds. 'But what we do is a lot more than sticking a label on a bottle. We offer a service that the companies want – to the client, good service is more important than the prices.' And nobody can complain when the service is perfect: 'We design the labels, we print them, we ship the champagne, we hold it in the warehouse free of charge, then send it out with compliment slips or whatever the client requires. It's all-encompassing,' explains Wilkinson.

The two of them are proof that to be successful you don't need to do it on your own: 'You are more likely to come to the right decision as a team,' says Wilson. 'I think it's important to work with someone else – to bounce ideas off each other. We also have an independent financial adviser who has been a tremendous help to us. Sometimes you need an outsider to tell you when you're wasting your time with some business.'

Wasting time does not come naturally to these two. They set targets and reach them: 'We have started from lowly beginnings and learnt the hard way and now those lessons are ingrained. When things pick up we're going to be laughing.' With a £270,000 turnover already achieved at a tender age, they're on target to make their first million soon. When lack of experience and money hasn't stopped them, there isn't much that will.

This is one hundred per cent proof-positive that even drink problems can turn into opportunities.

## Marco-Pierre White – The Recipe For Success

Marco-Pierre White is an Italian from a Yorkshire council house, where lads were supposed to drink beer, eat meat pies and do real men's jobs. Now he is one of Britain's most talented chefs and wealthiest entrepreneurs. The secret, he says, is simple: 'I just do things the way I've always wanted to do them. I've never allowed limits into my life.'

White says that by being independent you can avoid some of the things you don't like: 'I don't like snobbery and formality, for instance, so I won't have it my restaurant. Eating out, like life, is about enjoying yourself and being relaxed. You can't be successful unless you're the same way. With the restaurant, it's the food, the decor, everything. Just the same way as your attitude.'

White says that producing a good product is not enough, because people buy the whole ensemble. Although White's restaurant (Harvey's in South London) is expensive, all sorts of people go there. 'I make a point of never being rude or intimidating anyone. Value for money is top of the agenda – we're not cheap though, but our menus are written in English, because I like things which are understated. Before you can open up and enjoy yourself you've got to be relaxed. It takes confidence and you have to stop questioning yourself. You have to know you're good enough and not be afraid to do some self-promotion. Success is a very simple thing, really.'

One thing White hasn't mentioned is that he works very, very, hard. He regularly finishes at 5.00 am and starts back again at 9.00 am. He says he acquired these hard-working tendencies in Yorkshire: 'I was taught to work hard. My Mum died when I was 16 and my dad always told me to go into a profession, so I went into catering. When you're young you've got to work yourself hard. You've got to put in the foundations of success.'

'You don't need to be terrifically intelligent to be successful. Catering has a lot of people who are very bright without being intelligent. The most important thing is to have objectives. I wanted a two-star Michelin restaurant, so that's what I set out to achieve.' He did it within two and a half years and was the youngest ever person to win the Michelin stars.

According to White, the secret of success is being able to recognise your own weaknesses and turn them into advantages. 'My strengths are understanding my weaknesses – for instance, I'm a bit of a show-off.' He therefore applies this to his work and turns it into good presentation. 'Dealing with other people is most people's greatest weakness – it was certainly mine. I can be on my own at home and I'm not lonely but I hate eating alone in a restaurant. I think it's my insecurities that motivate me to be better. Most people are not whole people – they don't recognise their weaknesses and their negative points and work on them. That's what I do when I recruit staff. I turn their negatives into positives. They have to be honest with themselves. There's a lot of wealthy people in this world, but how many are happy with their success? Not many. You have to come to terms with yourself.'

Does everyone have the capacity to be successful? 'No, not everyone. Some just accept their life as it is. You have to be driven. A lot of successful people are.'

White says it's a big advantage being a Northerner: 'Northerners, generally, are very repressed. They very seldom praise each other. That's why I have a lot of waiters who come from council estates who are just like I was. You can bring them out of it. They often don't have the chances that Southerners do, so when they get an opportunity, they take it. My father's generation represented the tail end of Victorian England, which was founded on discipline, and Northerners have got that. Usually, they've also seen both sides of the fence and that's wonderful. I've lived in streets where everyone is a millionaire and I'd still rather talk to the ordinary people who come into the restaurant, because they're more interesting.'

White says it's all too easy for people to think they're worthless, because they can't find what they're good at. He thinks everyone can do something worthwhile, but not everyone finds it. 'You can't dismiss people, they're all equally worthwhile. I've never gone out of my way to cultivate people, I've just become familiar with them.'

His philosophy is the same as when he first started: 'Work hard, be brave and allow yourself no excuses. You have to learn to extend your capability.' He says many people are put off bettering themselves because of schools, and he still has a low opinion of teachers: 'I'd stuff all the teachers and put them in a glass box, because if they were really so good at their subject they'd be out there doing it, instead of teaching it.'

The other side of White is his Italian background. He loves families and good food: 'Families are very important. At one stage I was very ill and the people around me were really very supportive.' But his greatest inspiration is a Frenchman: Albert Roux, Head Chef at top London restaurant, Le Gavroche. 'He was my great model. He is very loyal and very strong. My advice is to always surround yourself with strong people, then you can't be afraid of hurting people's feelings. Weak people let you down. Strong people are at ease with themselves.'

There are pitfalls associated with success – 'Lots of people say how wonderful you are when you do well, but you mustn't be taken in by all that. I never pander to my ego. I'm not interested in what people say about me.

'Some people live for other people. They watch soap operas and think the actor's lives are more important than theirs. You have to be interested in yourself and be determined to succeed. For instance, if a plan collapses, as it occasionally has done in the past, I just rebuild it. The great thing about being from a poor background is that you don't feel as if you've got anything to lose. The worst thing that can happen is that I go back to a council house. Much as I like the North, I would not want my daughter to be brought up there. She might not be as strong. I was lucky to get out of it all and make a success.'

Keeping motivated is easy for White: 'My greatest love is still cooking. The day I stop doing that is the day everything starts to crumble.' It seems that keeping it on the boil is important in more ways than one.

# Appendix

To prove that you don't have to be a workaholic to succeed, people were asked what they would do with an extra day if they had one. The results are listed below:

**Brian Angliss** (owner of AC Cars which builds the AC Cobra sports car)
  'I'd go away from the business and spend the day at my house in Guernsey.'

**John Ashcroft** (businessman and ex-Chairman of Coloroll)
  'I'd spend it with my family.'

**Andy Brown** (MD of a marketing consultancy)
  'Nothing special – just spend it quietly with my girlfriend.'

**Shirley Conran** (best-selling author)
  'It's not something I can imagine, having an extra day, but if I could choose where to spend it I would go walking in the foothills of Tibet.'

**Bob Payton** (owner of My Kinda Town Restaurants)
  'Would probably watch American Football or go fox-hunting.'

**Michael Dell** (owner of Dell Computers)
  'I tend to think about business all the time in one way or another, so I could be doing anything and still have a good idea.'

**Daniel Field** (owner of chain of hairdressing salons)
  'I enjoy my work so much I don't like taking time off, and even

when I'm not talking about the business I'm thinking about it.'

**Sir Ranulph Fiennes** (explorer)
'I'd want to get away from it all. I'd be in my house on Exmoor (which has no modern facilities).'

**Richard Gabriel** (owner of Interlink)
'I would go flying in the helicopter or aeroplane, or drive the Bentley or the Aston Martin.'

**Tony Gordon** (one of the world's top insurance salesmen)
'What I would do depends on what challenge I face at the time. There are lots of different things I want to do with my spare time.'

**Kevin Harrington** (owner of Harrington Kilbride publishers)
'I love my work so I would probably spend it working. The evening would be more use. I would go to the theatre or maybe stay at home with a good bottle of wine.'

**John Harrison** (jungle explorer)
'I'd spend it writing up my adventures or putting up some shelves.'

**John Harvey-Jones** (ex-Chairman of ICI)
Does not like to waste time because 'If you're not making progress all the time, you're slipping backwards.' He would happily spend the extra day writing about business.

**Tony Hawser** (owner of Reject Shop)
'I don't know if I could get out to the States in a day, but I would rather spend the extra day there, in Maine.'

**Howard Hodgson** (millionaire from his (now sold) undertaking business)
'Well I'm spoilt for choice; any of the houses or the boat are nice, but they count for nothing without the family there as well.'

**Colin Jackson** (sprinter and athlete)
'An extra day would be the same for me as any other day. I'd still have to train – once I've done that I don't have a lot of energy for anything else.'

**Sophie Mirman** (ex-owner of Sockshop and businesswoman)

## The Unemployables

'I would ride, or play tennis or just walk the dog. It's so long since I did any of these I think I may have forgotten how.'

**David Northrop** (27-year-old bond-dealer turned restauranteur)
'Well, I'm still very young and there are a lot of things I'd like to do with an extra day, but I couldn't possibly fit them all in. You have to make a start somewhere and I'd like to learn to fly, therefore I'd do a day's flying. If did this every leap year, I might have learnt by the time I was seventy!'

**Peter Parfitt** (ex-Middlesex and England cricketer turned businessman)
'Oh, that's an easy question. I'd either play golf or watch cricket.'

**Jozsef Pinter** (Hungarian industrialist)
Would probably spend his day flying his aeroplanes or designing a new engineering project.

**Fiona Price** (businesswoman)
'I'd spend it riding or working on my book.'

**Alan Sugar** (founder and owner of Amstrad)
'Play tennis.'

**Sir Mark Weinberg** (businessman)
'I am interested, to the point of obsession, in computers but mainly I like pottering around on boats, going skiing, seeing friends or being with my family, so that's what I'd do.'

**The Unemployables Club**

The Unemployables Club is an informal group that meets once a quarter to discuss issues. Further details can be obtained from Jackie Pinnock at Lewis Consulting Group — tel. 0171-831 4890.

> ALSO AVAILABLE FROM MANAGEMENT BOOKS 2000

# The Superchiefs
## The People, Principles and Practice of the New Management Style
### Robert Heller

*(HB, £19.99, 336pp, 234mm x 156mm, ISBN: 1-85251-146-X)*

There is a new breed of dynamic managers at work – practising a new kind of dynamic management. *The Superchiefs* is the first account of the new management and the new managers in action – what they do, how they do it, and why. The reason lies above all in the mounting pace of change against a background of fast and furious competition. The old ways of top-down hierarchal management don't work any more. Chief executives have to change their styles, method and roles – to become less 'chief', less 'executive', far more effective. They can no longer try to run their companies as dominant power-houses of decision. Now their role is to unlock the power that exists lower down the corporation – all the way down.

All these vital initiatives have to be led from the top – but in doing so they change life at the top. They don't make that life any easier. For today's superchiefs have no guarantee of either success or permanence. One false step, and even a superbly managed growth star can stumble into loss, or worse. *The Superchiefs* studies the cautionary tales of failure as well as the inspiring story of success.

ABOUT THE AUTHOR
Robert Heller was the founding editor of *Management Today*, now Britains's leading monthly business magazine, and was also instrumental in the subsequent launch of *Campaign*, *Computing* and *Accountancy Age*. He has written many books, including *The Naked Manager* and *Culture Shock: The Office Revolution*. He is also editor of *The Complete Guide to Modern Management*, also published by Management Books 2000.

> *Available from leading booksellers.*
> *To order by phone, ring 01235-815544 now (credit cards accepted)*

> ALSO AVAILABLE FROM MANAGEMENT BOOKS 2000

# The How to Manage Handbook

## York Management Services

*(PB, £12.99, 220pp, 279mm x 210mm, ISBN: 1-85252-220-8)*

A virtual encyclopedia of management techniques – probably the most practical guide ever written for Managers.

This book provides hundreds of practical tips and sound advice on management and solving management problems along with motivational articles for managers and staff.

*The How to Manage Handbook* is free of superfluous management theory. Its easy to read format is comprehensive, yet concise. The subjects covered are presented under eight major headings:

- Developing Personal Skills
- Managing Your Team
- Managing Your Time
- The Art Of Communicating
- Organising Your Human Resources
- Dealing With The Personnel Issues
- Running Your Office
- Useful References

ABOUT THE AUTHOR
Compiled by York Management Services, an international consultancy.

**Concise, packed with information, and excellent value (220pp, large format @ £12.99)**

> *Available from leading booksellers.*
> To order by phone, ring 01235-815544 now (credit cards accepted)

*ALSO AVAILABLE FROM MANAGEMENT BOOKS 2000*

# Peak Performance
## Become More Effective at Work
### Windy Dryden

(PB, £9.99, 160pp, 234mm x 156mm, ISBN: 1-85252-182-1)

An innovative self-training book introducing a new system of personal development based on the pioneering principles of "Rational-Emotive Training".

This book introduces business executives and decision-makers in industry and government to a new research-tested way of thinking, feeling and acting, designed to maximise their executive ability to cope efficiently with the every day problems and hassles of the organisational world, and to operate both their business and personal life with minimum stress and maximum satisfaction.

*Peak Performance* will help readers to cut their way through the emotional problems and other personal pressures and blocks which get in the way of achieving optimum results for themselves and their organisations.

ABOUT THE AUTHOR
Windy Dryden is a senior lecturer in psychology at Goldsmiths' College, University of London. He has written or edited 40 books and over 120 articles and book chapters. He is Britain's leading counselling psychologist and counsellor educator.

Jack Gordon has worked in a variety of management jobs in government and private companies. He has trained in Rational-Emotive psychotherapy (RET) and has co-authored with Windy Dryden a practitioner's manual entitled "What is Rational-Emotive Therapy?"

**'Presents the principles and practices of rational emotive therapy (REP)'** *Business Executive*

*Available from leading booksellers.
To order by phone, ring 01235-815544 now (credit cards accepted)*

ALSO AVAILABLE FROM MANAGEMENT BOOKS 2000

# The Deming Management Method
## Mary Walton
*(PB, £9.99, 272pp, 229mm x 145mm, ISBN: 1-85252-141-4)*

Whether one is the owner of a small business, a middle manager in a medium-sized company, or the CEO of a multinational, this book demonstrates how to improve profits and productivity by following the principles of the Deming management method.

Middle- and top-echelon managers in particular will find *The Deming Management Method* provocative and controversial. Dr W Edwards, a noted statistician/management consultant, suggests a total revamping of the way managers manage. Change, Dr deming believes, starts at the top with an informed quality-conscious management. This book includes excellent advice on how to achieve that level of management expertise in the author's analysis of Dr Deming's famour 14 Points for Managers and his Deadly Diseases of Management.

ABOUT THE AUTHOR
Mary Walton is a staff writer for *The Philadelphia Inquirer Magazine*. She has spent much time with Dr Deming and has received his full co-operation, attending his seminars and interviewing him extensively.

'Lucid, practical and thoroughly convincing.' *Business*

*Available from leading booksellers.*
*To order by phone, ring 01235-815544 now (credit cards accepted)*

*ALSO AVAILABLE FROM MANAGEMENT BOOKS 2000*

# Running Your Own Business
## Robert Leach

*(PB, £9.99, 216pp, 234mm x 156mm, ISBN: 1-85252-187-2)*

This book combines practical reference information with management guidance directed at anyone running or setting up their own business. Subjects covered include:

- Is self-employment and business management for you?
- The rudiments of legal form, name and premises
- How to raise finance
- Basic accounting requirements and cash flow
- Tax and legal considerations
- Pension, insurance and banking arrangements
- The management skills necessary for entrepreneurial success

This book is part of a complete small business support package. By completing and sending to the publisher the registration form at the back of the book readers will receive **free updates** until 1995 when the next edition is planned. Registering for the book also entitles readers to a discount on certain training courses provided by *Dore International* and for *Business Bulletin*.

ABOUT THE AUTHOR
Robert Leach is a freelance financial writer and a qualified certified accountant with 15 years' experience of working in industry. He has been features editor of *The Accountant* and now writes regularly for the *Daily Telegraph* and other publications. He is also editor of many specialist works, including *The Auditor's Factbook* and *The Tax Factbook*, and is a contributor to the Chartered Accountants Taxation Service.

**Free update service until 1995**

*Available from leading booksellers.
To order by phone, ring 0235-815544 now (credit cards accepted)*